An Event-Based Science Module

TORNADO!

Student Edition

Russell G. Wright

Innovative Learning Publications®

Addison Wesley Longman
Menlo Park, California • Reading, Massachusetts • New York
Don Mills, Ontario • Wokingham, England • Amsterdam • Bonn
Paris • Milan • Madrid • Sydney • Singapore • Tokyo
Seoul • Taipei • Mexico City • San Juan

The developers of Event-Based Science have been encouraged and supported at every step in the creative process by the superintendent and board of education of Montgomery County Public Schools, Rockville, Maryland (MCPS). The superintendent and board are committed to the systemic improvement of science instruction, grades preK–12. EBS is one of many projects undertaken to ensure the scientific literacy of all students.

The developers of *Tornado!* pay special tribute to the editors, publisher, and reporters of the *Anniston Star* and *USA Today.* Without their cooperation and support, the creation of this module would not have been possible.

Cover Photograph: A. and J. Verkaik, The Stock Market

Pages 5, 11, 16, 21, 27, 29, 31, 34, 38, 46, 48, *USA Today;* pp. 11, 21, 34, 48, AP/Wide World Photos; p. 11, Joe McTyre, *Atlanta Journal Constitution*; pp. 11, 23, 26, 45, 49, 51, *Anniston Star*; p. 17, Thomas P. Grazulis, The Tornado Project; p. 23 (top), 25, Frank Loose; p. 40, Bill Mills; all Student Voices photos, Sherry Kughn.

Managing Editor: Cathy Anderson

Project Editor: Lois Fowkes

Production and Manufacturing Coordinator: Leanne Collins

Design Manager: Jeff Kelly

Text and Cover Design: Frank Loose Design

This book is published by Innovative Learning Publications®, an imprint of the Alternative Publishing Group of Addison Wesley Longman, Inc.

This material is based on work supported by the National Science Foundation under grant number MDR-9154094. Any opinions, findings, conclusions, or recommendations expressed in this publication are those of the Event-Based Science Project and do not necessarily reflect the views of the National Science Foundation.

Printed in the United States of America.

ISBN 0-201-49595-3

1 2 3 4 5 6 7 8 9 10-DR-00 99 98 97 96

Contents

Preface

The Event-Based Science Model

Tornado! is an earth-science module that follows the Event-Based Science (EBS) instructional model. You will watch "live" television news reports of the tornado that hit Piedmont, Alabama, on March 27, 1994. You will also read *USA Today* and *Anniston Star* reports about it. Your discussions about the tornado will show you and your teacher that you already know a lot about the earth-science concepts involved in the event. Next, a real-world task will put you and your classmates in the roles of people who must use scientific knowledge and processes to solve problems related to the severe weather threat. You will probably need more information before you start the task. *Tornado!* provides hands-on activities and a variety of reading materials to give you some of the background you need. About halfway through the unit, you will be ready to begin the task. Your teacher will assign you a role to play and turn you and your team loose to complete the task. You will spend the rest of the time in this module working on that task.

Scientific Literacy

A literate citizen is expected to know more than how to read, write, and do simple arithmetic. Today, literacy includes knowing how to analyze problems, ask critical questions, and explain events. A literate citizen must also be able to apply scientific knowledge and processes to new situations. Event-Based Science allows you to practice these skills by placing the study of science in a meaningful context.

Knowledge cannot be transferred to your mind from the mind of your teacher or from the pages of a textbook. Nor can knowledge occur in isolation from the other things you know about and have experienced in the real world. The Event-Based Science model is based on the idea that the best way to know something is to be actively engaged in it.

Therefore, the Event-Based Science model simulates real-life events and experiences to make your learning more authentic and memorable. First, the event is brought to life through television news coverage. Viewing the news allows you to be there "as it happened," and that is as close as you can get to actually experiencing the event. Second, by simulating the kinds of teamwork and problem solving that occur every day in our workplaces and communities, you will get a feeling for the role that scientific knowledge and teamwork play in the lives of ordinary people. Thus *Tornado!* is built around simulations of real-life events and experiences that affected people's lives and environments dramatically.

In an Event-Based Science classroom, you become the workers, your product is a solution to a real problem, and your teacher is your coach, guide, and advisor. You will be assessed on how you use scientific processes and concepts to solve problems as well as on the quality of your work.

One of the primary goals of the Event-Based Science Project is to place the learning of science in a real-world context and to make scientific learning fun. You should not allow yourself to become frustrated. If you cannot find a specific piece of information, it's okay to be creative. For example, if you are the duty forecaster responsible for recording warning announcements for broadcast over the weather radio, do not worry if you have never heard a real broadcast. Base your response on the real people and things you know about. When you write the script, you might also use some of the words used by television and radio weather forecasters in your community. Do not let yourself get bogged down in the details.

Student Resources

Tornado! is unlike a regular textbook. An Event-Based Science module tells a story about a real event; it has real newspaper articles about the event and inserts that explain the scientific concepts involved in the event. It also contains science activities for you to conduct in your science class and interdisciplinary activities that you may do in English, math, social studies, or technology education classes. In addition, an Event-Based Science module gives you and your classmates a real-world task to do. The task is always done by teams of students, with each team member performing a real-life role while completing an important part of the task. The task cannot be completed without you and everyone else on your team doing your parts. The team approach allows you to share your knowledge and strengths. It also helps you learn to work with a team in a real-world situation. Today, most professionals work in teams.

Interviews with people who actually serve in the roles you are playing are scattered throughout the Event-Based Science module. Middle-school students who actually experienced the event tell their stories throughout the module, too.

As this module is unlike a regular textbook, you have much more flexibility in using it.

- You may read **The Story** for enjoyment or to find clues that will help you tackle your part of the task.
- You may read selections from the **Discovery File** when you need help understanding something in the story or when you need help with the task.
- You may read all the **On the Job** features because you are curious about what professionals do, or you may read only the interview with the professional who works in the role you've chosen because it may give you ideas that will help you complete the task.
- You may read the **In the News** features because they catch your eye, or as part of your search for information.
- You will probably read all the **Student Voices** features because they are interesting stories told by middle-school students such as yourself.

Tornado! is also unlike a regular textbook in that the collection of resources found in it is not meant to be complete. You must find additional information from other sources, too. Textbooks, encyclopedias, pamphlets, magazine and newspaper articles, videos, films, filmstrips, computer databases, and people in your community are all potential sources of useful information. It is vital to your preparation as a scientifically literate citizen of the twenty-first century that you get used to finding information on your own.

The shape of a new form of science education is beginning to emerge, and the Event-Based Science Project is leading the way. We hope you enjoy your experience with this module as much as we enjoyed developing it.

—Russell G. Wright, Ed.D.
Project Director and Principal Author

The Story—Part 1

Palm Sunday

On March 27, 1994, a peaceful Palm Sunday service was transformed into a scene of horror.

Inside the Goshen United Methodist Church in southern Cherokee County just north of Piedmont, Alabama, a congregation of 140 people was holding a Palm Sunday service.

Suddenly, the lights flickered on and off. Moments later, the electricity completely failed. Despite the blackout, the choir director at the church began the next hymn. Surely the lights would come back on.

But outside the church, the wind howled. Roof shingles from nearby homes swirled through the air. Gusts of wind snapped off trees and downed telephone and electric lines. Storm clouds billowed and a large, dark, funnel-like cloud raced across grassy hills near the church.

A police officer spotted the rotating funnel cloud stretching to the ground from a mass of dark clouds. It was heading toward the church. He excitedly radioed in a report to police headquarters in Piedmont. But the storm was moving fast. There was not enough time to warn the people singing hymns in Goshen United Methodist Church.

The worshipers heard a roaring sound first, followed by the noise of broken glass as windows blew in. The choir's singing abruptly stopped. Screams and children's cries filled the air, mixed with shouts of "Get down! Get down!" Some ducked under benches. Others tried to scramble for safety. It was too late for all to escape. The time was 11:39 A.M.

Within seconds, powerful gusts collapsed large segments of the building's brick walls. Without support, the church roof fell. A downpour of glass, brick, and wood swirled through the pews.

Student Voices

The wind was blowing like an ordinary thunderstorm. There was a dark bluish-greenish-purplish look to the sky. My dog, Shatsi, was whining. She stays outside, so she knows how things are supposed to be. Shatsi knew it was not normal. She knew something was going on. I don't know how dogs have that sense, but they do.

David Murphy
Piedmont, Alabama

Moving away from the wreckage of the church, the thick, swirling funnel cloud continued on its path of destruction.

The tornado had killed 20 church members and injured 90. The 40-year-old church was demolished. State troopers, police, and townspeople hurriedly searched the jumble of debris. Cranes were brought in to lift the roof. Rescuers worked in the pelting rain with chain saws and with their bare hands to clear away other wreckage.

Those who survived the ordeal were pulled from the rubble and rushed to the hospital. Many suffered severe injuries. The dead were removed from the wreckage and placed in a temporary morgue—a tornado-damaged house across the street from the church.

The local National Guard armory also became a makeshift morgue where the sad ordeal of identifying the dead began. Piedmont's civic center gymnasium served as shelter for tornado victims. People from miles around rushed to the civic center with supplies to help survivors. Simple things—blankets, towels, and food—were very valuable.

The Goshen tornado was only one of about 30 in the system that struck four states. One local newspaper, the *Anniston Star*, termed the tragedy "Tornado Sunday." As time moved on, the true scope of Tornado Sunday became more apparent. In total, 23 Alabamans lost their lives due to the Goshen tornado; 157 were injured. The tornado demolished more than 100 houses and about 275 mobile homes. It damaged another 1,052 houses and 17 mobile homes. About 86 businesses were completely destroyed or damaged. An early estimate of the tornado devastation was put at $20 million in repair costs.

In an instant, the quiet community of Goshen had become the subject of headlines across the country as the place hit hardest by the March 27 calamity.

Discussion Questions

- **What are tornadoes and what causes them?**
- **What is it about your part of the country that accounts for the fact that you (pick one) (a) frequently, (b) occasionally, (c) seldom, or (d) never experience tornadoes?**
- **Other forms of violent weather affect your region. Make a list of the violent storms and other weather events that your region experiences. Rank them in order from the most frequent to the least frequent.**
- **What is the most important way weather affects your life?**

IN THE NEWS

Goshen United Methodist part of the history of an old town

By Eric Larson
Star Religion Writer

GOSHEN — In the Biblical account of the events leading to the first Passover, Yahweh sent a plague of hail upon Egypt but spared the land of Goshen.

Goshen was not spared on Sunday when storms ripped through the community, leveling the United Methodist Church.

Church members, reeling from the loss of at least 21 of their congregation, vowed to maintain their church.

"We've still got a church. We just don't have a building," church member Harold Price, 80, said early this morning.

The building was relatively new as country churches go, built in 1951.

The church's directory provides a history: The original building was on the Old Centre Highway, now Cherokee County 31. The church was chartered as part of the Methodist Episcopal Church South in 1905 with 35 members.

Those members came from the Mountain Springs Methodist Church on the Centre Circuit. Its first pastor was the Rev. Charles W. Seale.

"This was not the first church in the community," said Margaret Stewart, a historian who lives just yards from church, on the same land that the first Stewarts did. "The Methodists were more or less late-comers for this area."

The first people in the area were native Cherokee. Goshen first appeared on the map of Benton County in 1832 when a post office was instituted, Mrs. Stewart said. In 1836, the little town became part of Cherokee County upon a treaty with the Indians. There's still controversy today over whether the town is part of Cherokee County or Calhoun County, according to Mrs. Stewart.

The community's name comes from books of the Old Testament. When famine ravaged the land of Canaan, the Egyptian ruler Joseph invited the people of Israel to settle in Goshen where they could — and did — prosper.

The early years of the church saw the congregation grow to 50 or 60 people, Price said. On Sunday afternoons, a pastor from a Methodist church in Piedmont conducted services. Full-time pastors rarely stayed more than one or two years.

Since Rev. Kelly Clem arrived four years ago, the church has experienced "tremendous growth," Price said. Average attendance has been 120. More than that were there for Palm Sunday services, celebrating Jesus's entrance to Jerusalem on a donkey.

"I don't think God designed anything like a cyclone to come around and knock our church down," Price said. "It was an act of nature, and we happened to be in the wrong place at the wrong time."

ANNISTON STAR, MONDAY, MARCH 28, 1994

DISCOVERY FILE

Wind

The air surrounding the earth is almost always in motion. When it moves slowly, we call that movement a breeze. When it moves so fast we cannot stand up, we call it a *gale* or *hurricane*. When air swirls around and around so fast that it picks up cars and drops them miles away, we call it a *tornado*.

But what makes the wind blow at all? To understand the answer, keep in mind this basic principle: warm air rises and expands, because when air is warmed, the air molecules move faster and spread out. Air molecules found above cold surfaces slow down and are much more closely packed together. So hot air is less dense and therefore lighter than the same amount of cold air at the same level.

Now, imagine the sun as it travels across the sky. As it passes over the earth, it warms some spots more than others. Dark surfaces absorb more of the sun's energy than do light-colored surfaces. As energy is absorbed, the temperature rises. The air above these hot spots rises, too, and cool air rushes in to fill the void. This kind of movement is called *convection*.

As convection continues, an area of low pressure forms under the rising warm air. High pressure forms under the sinking cooler air. This difference of density and pressure over continents and oceans and between hot and cold regions makes the air move and thus starts the winds blowing.

Imagine, for example, the temperature differences between the equator and the poles. As you might expect, the warm air at the equator tends to rise and be replaced by cold air moving in underneath it from the poles. These pressure differences create a general movement of air worldwide. This global air movement provides a moderating effect on the otherwise extreme temperatures at the equator and the poles.

Why do global winds tend to circle around the globe rather than flowing in straight lines from the poles to the equator? The winds are turned by the Coriolis effect. Nineteenth-century French scientist G. G. Coriolis observed that, because of the earth's rotation, winds in the Northern Hemisphere are deflected to the right while those in the Southern Hemisphere are deflected to the left. It is this Coriolis force that explains why the air in certain air masses, including high-pressure masses, spins in a clockwise direction in the Northern Hemisphere and in a counterclockwise direction in the Southern Hemisphere. Coriolis noted that the faster the wind is moving, the greater the deflection.

A complicated interaction between the Coriolis force and the force of the pressure itself causes low-pressure air masses to spin the opposite direction of high-pressure ones—counterclockwise in the Northern Hemisphere and clockwise in the Southern Hemisphere. Much of the earth's weather depends on a system of winds that blow in more or less expected directions.

You have probably heard of the jet stream, a narrow band of high-altitude wind that blows from west to east at about 60 miles per hour in the summer and at about 150 miles per hour in the winter—a time when there is a great temperature con-

➤ continued on page 4

STUDENT VOICES

The people in the church—I just don't see how they handled it as well as they did. One boy who goes to another school lost his dad and sister. His mother was in the hospital for months. I heard about this from my friends at the other school.

ASHLEY HUNT
PIEDMONT, ALABAMA

➤ continued from page 3

trast between the polar regions and more temperate areas. The jet stream does not circle the poles smoothly but loops down into more temperate zones, sometimes bringing air from the North Pole almost as far south as the tropics.

In tropical regions about 20 to 30 degrees north and south of the equator, there is often only a slight breeze. What wind there is changes direction often. These almost windless areas, called the *doldrums,* were dangerous when ships relied on wind to sail the seas. Ships could be stranded for weeks.

Sailors of old called these belts of calm high-pressure air circling the globe the Horse Latitudes. It seems that horses sometimes died of thirst when the sailing ships carrying them languished for lack of wind.

Land breezes and sea breezes are local winds. During the day, the land warms up more than the sea. The warm air rises and the cooler air over the sea flows in to replace it. At night, the pattern is reversed. The land cools more quickly than the water, so the warmer air over the sea rises, and cooler air from land flows out to replace it. This flow of air from land to sea is called a *land breeze.*

Another local wind system is a *mountain wind.* Mountain slopes, especially those made of bare rock, are heated by the sun during the day. The warm air rises, and more air flows upward from valleys to fill its place. This creates an updraft along the sides of mountains during the afternoon. The reverse occurs at night, as the mountain slope cools, and heavier cold air flows back down into the valleys.

Thunderstorms and tornadoes are local winds too. Can you explain the winds in a thunderstorm?

DISCOVERY FILE

Myths About the Wind

Even early humans wondered why the winds blow. Ancient Greeks believed that Aeolus—the god of winds—created storms, hurricanes, and other wild weather. Legend claims Aeolus kept the winds locked in a cave with eight openings. Each opening was blocked by a large rock. When Aeolus chose to roll one of the rocks away, the escaping winds would create a cool summer breeze or a raging hurricane. Native Americans of the eastern woodland tribes, as well as the ancient Greeks, believed their gods could control the wind. In early times in Scotland, witches claimed to be able to raise the wind.

Famous Greek philosopher Aristotle classified winds as being either polar or equatorial. Living more than 2,000 years ago without the aid of modern weather-monitoring technology or satellite data, he described with accuracy the kind of weather each wind would bring.

About two centuries ago, Benjamin Franklin also studied the winds. Though belief at the time was to the contrary, he noted that wind moves from west to east. Because his observations were valuable to farmers and sailors, he published them in *Poor Richard's Almanac.*

Over the years, inventors have tried to come up with ways to subdue wild winds. In 1886, John B. Atwater patented a device called the "cyclone destroyer." Explosives were used to try to break up the force of the winds.

The wind has also been the subject of a number of famous songs. To name a few: "Running against the Wind" by Bob Seger, "Summer Breeze" by Loggins and Messina, "Blowin' in the Wind" by Bob Dylan, "Dust in the Wind" by Kansas, and the folk song "They Call the Wind Mariah."

DISCOVERY FILE

Chinooks and Wind Chill: Blowing Hot and Cold

Chinooks are warm, dry winds that can melt a foot of snow in less than an hour. They are found flowing downslope in the Rocky Mountains. According to tradition, the Indian word *chinook* means "snow eater."

In California, these warm, strong downslope winds are called Santa Ana winds. When a brushfire breaks out in Southern California, the Santa Ana winds flowing off the coastal range can make fighting fires extremely difficult. Santa Ana winds often cause wildfires to grow out of control.

Wind chill is a measure of how cold exposed skin actually feels. A combination of wind and cold causes a body to lose heat faster than cold temperatures alone. It is the speed with which our bodies lose heat that gives us the feeling of being cold. The faster the heat loss, the colder we feel. Wind chill temperatures are meaningful to people and other living things. Wind chill also affects objects such as cars and houses. The main dangers of exposure to extreme cold are hypothermia and frostbite. These dangers are increased by the wind.

Here's how wind chill works. Your body is constantly struggling to keep your internal temperature close to 98.6 °F. That is called *homeostasis.* As heat escapes from your body, the air next to you is warmed. If the air next to you is still, the warm air surrounds you and your body does not have to work as hard to keep warm. Wind blows this warm layer away.

Skin can actually freeze. When that happens, sharply pointed ice crystals form in the skin that can severely damage tissue. This is called *frostbite.* Your ears, nose, hands, and feet are the most vulnerable to frostbite.

In addition, if you are wearing wet clothes, the chilling effect of the wind greatly increases. Wind speeds the evaporation of moisture, and evaporation cools your body. In hot weather, we sweat to keep cool.

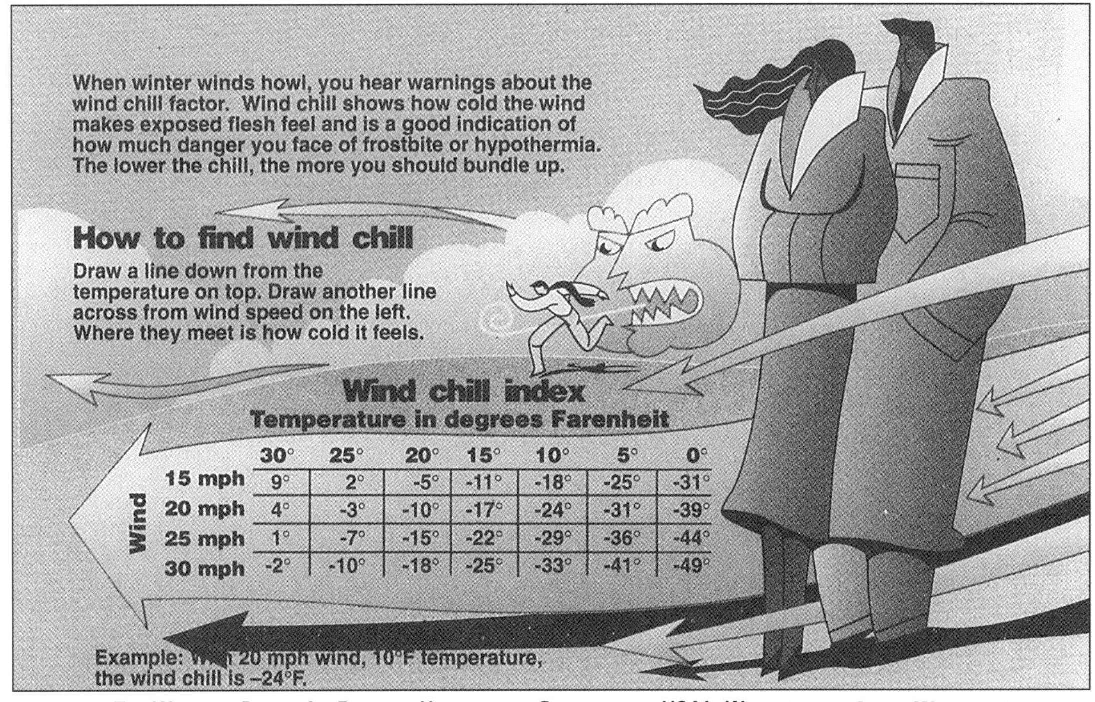

Wind	30°	25°	20°	15°	10°	5°	0°
15 mph	9°	2°	-5°	-11°	-18°	-25°	-31°
20 mph	4°	-3°	-10°	-17°	-24°	-31°	-39°
25 mph	1°	-7°	-15°	-22°	-29°	-36°	-44°
30 mph	-2°	-10°	-18°	-25°	-33°	-41°	-49°

SOURCE: *THE WEATHER BOOK: AN EASY-TO-UNDERSTAND GUIDE TO THE USA'S WEATHER,* BY JACK WILLIAMS, 1992, P. 26. *USA TODAY.*

DISCOVERY FILE

Air Is Pushing You Down

Air Pressure

It may be hard to believe, but the weight of the atmosphere is constantly pressing on you. At sea level, every square inch of your skin receives approximately 14.7 pounds of pressure. There is less pressure at higher elevations. At 18,000 feet, the pressure has dropped to 7.3 pounds per square inch.

When we rise from sea level to 18,000 feet we do not notice this change in pressure on our skin, but we do notice it other ways. Our eardrums are especially sensitive to rapid changes in air pressure as we drive up a mountain or climb higher in an airplane. What causes air pressure, and what does it have to do with weather?

Though you cannot see it, air takes up space and has mass. Things that take up space and have mass are called *matter,* and matter is made of molecules. Air molecules, mostly nitrogen and oxygen, are moving about at incredible speeds all around us. In fact, near the earth's surface, they are traveling at more than 1,000 miles per hour. The impact of all those molecules zipping around at such high speeds is what causes pressure. The more collisions, the higher the pressure. We don't feel this high-speed bombardment as wind, because the molecules are moving in different directions. In fact, we don't even feel the bombardment as pressure unless it changes suddenly. To understand how air pressure is related to weather, read the Discovery File about wind on page 3.

The Barometer

You can measure air pressure using a mercury barometer—one of the great scientific innovations of the Renaissance. It was invented in 1643 by Evangelista Torricelli, one of Galileo's assistants. Today's mercury barometer has changed little since the days of Torricelli.

Torricelli took a tube, closed one end, and filled it with mercury. He then placed it open end down in a dish of mercury. Air pressure on the mercury in the container kept the mercury from flowing down into the dish. And as the air pressure increased, it would press down harder on the mercury in the dish, forcing it higher into the tube. He attached a ruler to the tube to measure the height of the mercury. Extremely high pressure at sea level can push the mercury up to about 32 inches in the tube.

A barometer is probably the most useful instrument for forecasting weather. As the mercury in a barometer falls, you will know that low pressure and a likelihood of rain are in the forecast. A rise in air pressure fore-

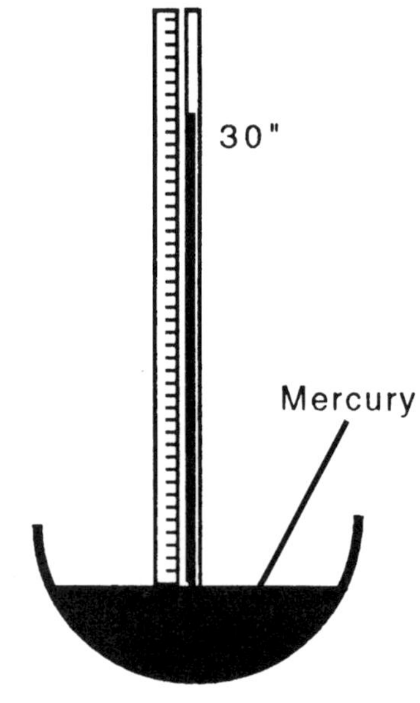

casts good weather. The unit of metric measurement of atmospheric pressure is the millibar. One millibar is equal to the pressure of $\frac{1}{32}$ of an inch of mercury. At sea level, the pressure is usually about 1,013 millibars. According to several barometers in Homestead, Florida, when Hurricane Andrew passed over, the atmospheric pressure measured only 926 millibars. The lower the barometric pressure, the stronger the storm.

Science Activity

Weather in a Box

Purpose

To demonstrate the movement of weather fronts using water masses of different temperatures.

Background

A television production company is filming a segment about severe weather for a kids' show. They have hired you and your team to build a three-dimensional working model showing how weather fronts move. Since water and air are both fluids and flow in similar ways, you plan to use water for the demonstration.

Materials

For each group:

- Clear plastic box or aquarium
- 3 or more plastic cups
- Scissors or other device to put holes in cups
- Masking tape or duct tape
- Blue and red food coloring
- Ice
- Stopwatch or other timing device
- File folder for portfolio
- Other experimenting materials as needed

For the class:

- Hot water
- Video recorder or chart materials

Procedure

Before you begin, you will need to assign jobs within your group. One person will pour colored water, another person will measure the time needed for the water to move, and observers will describe the boundary of colored water from several points of view.

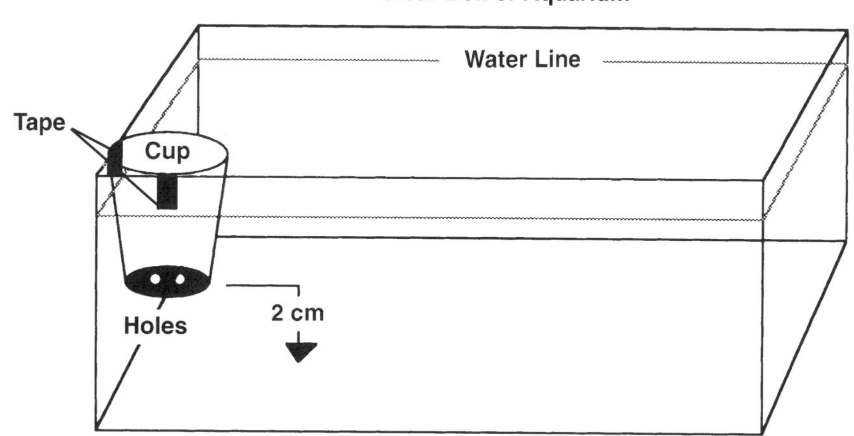

1. Punch some holes in the bottom of a plastic cup. Use masking tape or duct tape to fasten the cup to one corner of the box so that the bottom of the cup is about 2 centimeters above the bottom of the box.
2. Fill the plastic box with warm or hot water to within 1 centimeter of the top of the cup. Prepare a sample of blue-colored ice water in another cup.
3. Pour the blue ice water into the cup with the holes all at once. Watch carefully! After the trial, collect all written observations and data in a portfolio.
4. Repeat the procedure, looking for more details.
5. Brainstorm with your group about other materials you could use for other trials. Let your teacher know what you need. Run several experiments of your own design and then choose the one you will demonstrate. Explain what your demonstration shows about fronts. Be sure to use words that young children will understand.

Conclusion

You have observed front boundaries under several conditions. Select the conditions that gave you the best results. Write a short script that explains how what is happening in the box simulates what happens when air masses collide. If you have access to video equipment, videotape your demonstration. If no video equipment is available, you can prepare a live presentation. Use diagrams and charts as needed. For example, you might develop a series of diagrams that show what you observed at different points. Use data and observations from your portfolio to help you develop these charts and diagrams.

On the Job

Meteorologist in Charge

Antonio Alcides "Al" Dreumont
National Weather Service Forecast Office
Austin/San Antonio, Texas

I became interested in meteorology in high school when I had to do a term paper. I was searching for ideas at the library when a book on hurricanes caught my eye. Reading about lightning in hurricanes really "sparked" my interest.

Back then, pilots and meteorologists were just beginning to fly into hurricanes. These first "hurricane hunters" used small planes with special weather-monitoring instruments. In those days, hurricane hunting was more of an art than a science. It was more for thrills than for forecasting storms.

In the army, I was in artillery. To hit a target, we had to consider the "winds aloft." We learned to calculate the effect of wind speed and direction on the trajectory (or curve of the flight path) of an artillery shell.

It was my job to get the wind data from the base meteorologists. While visiting the base weather station, I thought, "Wow! This has got to be a neat way to make a living." I told my dad I wanted to be a meteorologist. He said, "Son, study something like engineering. You can earn a living in engineering. You're going to starve studying meteorology." How wrong he was! It's been a good career.

I earned my meteorology degree from Texas A & M University. After that, I went to work for the National Weather Service (NWS). It was called the Event Weather Bureau at that time.

One of the biggest problems in our area is flash flooding. We have tropical weather here. It's not uncommon for us to get 8 to 12 inches of rain overnight, sometimes even more. Flash floods can kill people.

As you and your team are working on the Task for this unit, try to imagine what it's really like at a NWS Forecast Office when there's a severe storm in the neighborhood. Here are some things to think about.

If I'm not snooping at the computers myself, my staff lets me know when a severe-storm, tornado, or flash-flood watch has been issued. The first thing I do is call the lead forecaster in the threatened area. I advise him or her that a watch is in effect.

I ask the forecaster these questions: Is your staff ready? Have you practiced all your drills? Do you know the procedures? Have you checked with the emergency-management coordinators in your county?

I'm also talking to emergency-management people at the State Department of Public Safety. I'm on the phone almost 80 percent of the time.

The lead forecaster is the leader, checking everything. The journey forecaster keeps track of the event as it unfolds minute by minute on the radar screen. The hydrometeorological technician (hydromet tech) examines the wind, barometric pressure, and humidity data flooding in.

As a thunderstorm develops, the team watches it very closely.

They are looking for those thunderstorms that are not behaving themselves. Storms with rotating winds inside are becoming severe. When a storm becomes severe, it tells us so. It reaches very high into the atmosphere—10 to 20 kilometers (6 to 12 miles). It has hail. And from the wind data, they can tell it is becoming a tornado. In other words, they have a problem on their hands. At that moment, things really jump into high gear.

At the moment a forecast office recognizes all the signs, it issues a tornado warning—a statement that lets the public know a tornado has been spotted. It takes a minute or less to record a warning and put it out over the weather radio and the satellite system. The warning is received by emergency-management people and the news media. If it were not for broadcast radio and television folks, the Weather Service couldn't reach nearly enough people. We have a beautiful partnership with them.

Once everyone has been notified, the forecasters sit back and watch the storm. There is absolutely nothing they can do to stop it. However, while watching the event, the staff is looking for changes to report and for things they have not noticed before. These little "discoveries" sometimes become the seeds for research projects by lead forecasters and hydromet techs. Hydrometeorological technicians do not have college degrees, but they are very knowledgeable and experienced. This gives them an opportunity to do research and receive some of the glory that goes with being a coauthor of a published research paper.

Lead forecasters and hydromet techs work on research papers on their own time without pay. In meteorology, we give the taxpayers more than their money's worth.

I've spoken at many schools. I look the students in the eye and say, "Do you have a genuine interest in science and mathematics? Are you interested in earth science—something you can really put your hands on, and feel, and look at, and experience? If you have these interests, why don't you try meteorology?"

Everyone is welcome at the NWS, regardless of ethnic background, gender, or physical ability. All we want is your brain—and your dedication to working in a field you enjoy. If your degree qualifies you to be a meteorologist, the NWS is there to hire you.

The NWS is a very good employer, but it is not the only one in our field. Meteorologists are also hired by airlines, the military, television stations, and private companies.

NWS hires people who have just earned their degrees. They work for two to three years as interns. The better grades they earned in college, the higher their starting salary as interns. If you have a 3.0 grade-point average, you start at the highest salary. We know that some students have to work while they are in college. It is hard to keep your grades up. So even if you do not have top grades, there are still opportunities for you.

If you have an interest in meteorology, I would suggest asking a parent or adult guardian to drive you over to the nearest National Weather Service Forecast Office for a visit. See what the office looks like. Talk to the meteorologist.

I have weather-monitoring equipment in my backyard. I measure temperature and rainfall. If you want to put up some weather-monitoring equipment in your backyard, here are a few suggestions. Start with thermometers and rain gauges. They are inexpensive. You can find weather equipment at pilots' shops near small local airports. Two other sources are livestock-feed stores and science education supply companies. Your local NWS office can sometimes provide a list of suppliers. Get your science teacher involved. Sometimes your teachers can get funds or equipment donated to the school.

Set up a small network with other students or community members to monitor the rainfall in your area. Each student can measure rainfall in a backyard gauge shortly after each storm. Every week, a different student can gather the data. After a few weeks, you can begin drawing maps of total precipitation in your area. Totals can vary greatly. This kind of research is fascinating.

We have volunteers who have weather-monitoring equipment, too. They call in their measurements to their local NWS forecast office. Some families have been calling in their measurements for 40 years.

The NWS Spotters Program is another volunteer program. Spotters report valuable observations that help save lives. Many of them are also HAM radio operators.

SCIENCE ACTIVITY

Daily Weather Map

Purpose

To follow the movement of weather across the United States in order to make a prediction.

Materials

For each group:

- 1 week of daily weather maps from a local newspaper or *USA Today*
- 2 outline maps of the United States (from the teacher)
- File folder

Background

A weather reporter for a local newspaper called yesterday. It seems the newspaper's editor wants to run a series of articles on weather forecasting. The series will include several activities for kids. They are especially concerned about one particular activity. Will it work?

They want their readers to observe the movement of weather patterns across the United States for one week and then forecast the weekend weather. Weather moves from west to east, so it should be an easy matter to use the movement to make the forecast. Right?

As a meteorologist for the United States Weather Service in Kansas City, Missouri, you know weather forecasting is complicated. There is much more to it than just tracking the movement of pressure systems and fronts and using those observations to predict the weather. But it just might work well enough.

The reporter wants you to try out the same procedures they will print in the newspaper and let them know whether you are satisfied.

The reporter has suggested the five steps listed on the sheet below.

Conclusion

Complete the activity exactly as written. Keep your records in a folder. After you make your prediction, tell the reporter how it worked. Prepare a brief reply in the form of a facsimile (fax). Be sure to invite the reporter to sit down with you to discuss the results.

Think about these questions as you write your reply:

1. What did you predict, and what actually happened?
2. Was your prediction close enough that you would recommend publishing the activity?
3. Do you recommend any changes or additions to the procedures?
4. Weather generally moves from west to east over the United States. Did your observations support this statement?

Predicting the Weather

1. Observe the United States weather map in your local newspaper each day for five days, starting on a Monday.
2. Record daily weather information in some organized way. Information such as the position and movement of pressure systems and fronts, daily high and low temperature, cloud cover, precipitation, and so on are possibilities. Record anything you decide may be helpful in predicting the weekend weather. (A collection of the maps themselves might help.)
3. On Friday, examine all of the information you have collected. Look for patterns in the movement of weather systems. How fast are the systems moving? In what direction are they moving? You are now ready to predict the weekend weather.
4. On the two outline maps of the United States, indicate where you think pressure systems and fronts will be located for Saturday and Sunday. Prepare your prediction for Kansas City.
5. Save your local newspaper's weekend weather maps to compare with your predictions. Also, record in a table the actual Kansas City weather for Saturday and Sunday. Be sure to include high and low temperature, cloud cover, and precipitation.

IN THE NEWS

Day of prayer turns to terror

Ala. church can only ask 'Why?'

By Tom Watson and Mimi Hall
USA TODAY

PIEDMONT, Ala. — Early Sunday, the radio carried weather warnings: Heavy storms were on the way.

But this was Palm Sunday, the day of the children's service at Goshen United Methodist Church. And so 140 worshipers, many wearing their Easter outfits, came to the sanctuary, ignoring the gathering clouds.

They sang, even after rising winds knocked the power out.

But suddenly, in the middle of the children's play, "things started hitting the side of the church, and something came through one of the windows," said Carol Scroggins, who was at the altar when the tornado hit. "I just started to scream, 'Everybody get down!' ... People were screaming, but it happened so quickly there wasn't much time for reaction."

When it was over, 17 bodies — six of them children — were pulled from the rubble of the toppled steeple, bricks and smashed pews. Two more victims died later. Ninety people were hurt, many with severe back and chest injuries; some reached hospitals in cars flagged down by survivors.

The devastation was part of a series of powerful twisters that wreaked havoc across the South on Sunday, killing at least 36 and destroying homes in Georgia, Alabama, North Carolina and South Carolina.

"One of the worst ones I've seen, one of the worst ones this century," was how Joe Wheeler, meteorologist at the National Weather Service in Birmingham, described it.

In Piedmont, a town of 5,000, the tornado seemed to skip over rooftops until its violent descent on Goshen United.

A hundred people, many who came from their own church services, arrived to sift through debris by hand as cranes lifted fallen beams. A morgue was set up at the local National Guard Armory. Among the dead was the daughter of Goshen's minister, Kelly Clem.

Other towns across the South also struggled to pick up the pieces Sunday night:

▶ In the small college town of Boiling Springs, N.C., "everything got real dark" as an afternoon tornado "tore up a lot of buildings and trees and all kinds of stuff," said Jimmy Ledford, owner of Ledford's Buy and Sell.

At Gardner-Webb College, cars flipped over, and the tornado damaged student dormitories and the library.

▶ In Charlotte, N.C., an evening tornado touched down at Douglas International Airport and a housing complex. One man was killed by lightning.

▶ Outside Ohatchee, Ala., a tornado damaged the Ten Island Baptist Church and injured some worshipers.

▶ In Guntersville, Ala., the roof was blown off a nursing home, and 25 to 30 residents — none of whom were injured — at the Marshall Manor Nursing Home were taken to Guntersville Hospital.

▶ In Ragland, Ala., a community near Piedmont, one woman died and 38 families were left homeless. Eight more were injured — mostly broken bones and cuts — in the storm that damaged houses, mobile homes, a service station and a Baptist church.

The devastation in Piedmont, where severe tornado warnings were issued again Sunday night, has stunned every household.

But residents like Fay Studdard say the town — and Goshen United — will survive and rebuild.

Linda Kanamine contributed

▶ Tornadoes hit, 1A

By Eddie Motes, AP
HELPING OUT: Rescuers help the injured at Goshen United Methodist Church in Piedmont, Ala. About 140 worshipers were present when the tornado struck.

By Joe McTyre, Atlanta Journal Constitution
CLEANUP WORK: Neighbors help remove possessions from a house in Tallulah Falls, Ga.

DEADLY TORNADOES

Nov. 21-23, 1992: 94 twisters kill 26 in 13 states from Texas to Virginia, Ohio and Indiana.

April 26-27, 1991: 54 tornadoes kill 21 people from Texas into Nebraska and Iowa.

May 31, 1985: 41 tornadoes kill 75 people in Ohio and Pennsylvania.

March 28, 1984: 22 tornadoes hit North Carolina and South Carolina, killing 57.

April 3-4, 1974: The most damaging outbreak in U.S. history. 127 tornadoes kill 315 people and injure 6,142 in 11 states from Indiana and Ohio into Alabama and Virginia. Downtown Xenia, Ohio, is destroyed.

April 11-12, 1965: 51 tornadoes hit Indiana, Ohio, Michigan, Wisconsin, Illinois in the Palm Sunday Outbreak; 271 dead, 1,600 hurt.

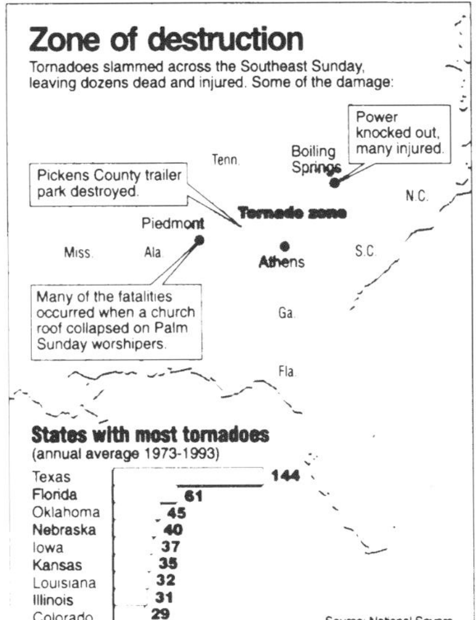

By Marty Baumann, USA TODAY

By Ken Elkins, Anniston Star via Reuters
DARK SEARCH: Rescuers look for survivors in the Goshen United Methodist Church. The storm struck during a children's play.

By Trent Penny, Anniston Star via AP
AFTERMATH: A pickup sits in a swimming pool of a demolished home in Jacksonville, Ala. Twisters wreaked havoc in the South.

USA TODAY, MONDAY, MARCH 28, 1994

Staffing a Forecast Office

The following appeared in the *Anniston Star*, Monday, March 28, 1994:

> OHATCHEE: Ken Ingram sifted through the rubble of Ten Island Baptist Church this morning, constantly shaking his head in amazement.
>
> The clock on a rear wall was frozen at 11:06 A.M. That's when 60 parishioners, who were about to sing their first hymn of the morning Sunday, heard the roar.
>
> "It sounded like a freight train coming," said Ingram, relating the words of his wife.
>
> The parishioners scrambled down a pair of stairways into the basement seconds before a tornado rumbled across Alabama Highway 77, wiping out a pine forest and shredding the church. According to Ingram, aside from a few cuts and bruises, no one was hurt.

As you will read in this module, others were not as fortunate as these 60 survivors. The tornadoes seemed to hit suddenly. Warnings had been sent out, but not everyone heard them. And not everyone knew what to look for in the sky to tell whether a tornado might form. At the National Weather Service Forecast Office for the region, a team of meteorologists had been examining the rush of data. They were looking for signs of severe thunderstorms and tornadoes. They knew something could happen, and it did.

STUDENT VOICES

The sky turned pitch black. The wind started picking up. I started getting scared. The wind was blowing hard and it was loud; it sounded like a whistle.

We have been closer to God since the tornado, because anything in life can happen. My house and my things, my friends—it can all be taken so easily. One of my friends I had known since kindergarten was killed in the Goshen church.

JEREMY PENNY
JACKSONVILLE, ALABAMA

The Forecasting Office

For this module, you and your coworkers will be inside one of six National Weather Service Forecast Offices in the Midwest. A tornado watch is already in effect for your area. Instrument readings and radar data reveal a rapidly changing situation.

The job of your forecast office is to issue short-range forecasts for the region. You must be ready to issue a warning if a severe thunderstorm or tornado actually occurs. You have also been asked to prepare a three-dimensional model of the atmosphere. The model should show weather that accompanies the passage of a cold front. Your finished model will be placed in the lobby of your forecast office so visiting school groups can better visualize the atmosphere near a severe thunderstorm.

Over the next few weeks, you and the other members of your team will learn about severe weather events. When you are ready to handle the job, a tornado watch will be issued, and you will receive hour-by-hour data on approaching storms. Data will come fast and heavy. There will be little time to stop and learn anything new. So before the watch is issued, learn all you can.

Everyone on your team needs to have the following knowledge and skills:

- how to read a weather radar screen
- how to read the symbols on a weather map
- how to use map and radar information to predict the weather
- when to issue a warning

The Task begins when a severe weather watch is issued by the National Severe Storms Forecast Center and your team is given the first hour's weather data. If you have questions about how to use radar-screen and weather-map data, tell your teacher what you need to know before you can start. During the Task, you will have a special role to play as part of the Weather Service staff. Examine the roles below and be prepared to apply for the job that best matches your qualifications.

After the severe weather passes, you and your team will prepare a written evaluation of your performance. How did you do? Did you see a tornado in time to warn communities in its path? If not, did you learn anything that could help you next time? Your evaluation will be the final product for this module.

The Roles

Your team's lead forecaster (LF) is the leader. The LF coordinates the work of the team and has final responsibility for the forecast issued to the public. The LF will also supervise completion of the three-dimensional model and final event evaluation.

The science and operations officer (SOO) is the person most familiar with the processes that go on inside a severe thunderstorm. This person works with colleagues and the public to show the science behind weather occurrences in the region. Design and construction of the model is the primary responsibility of the SOO.

The warnings-coordination meteorologist (WCM) is responsible for communicating weather information to the public in words everyone understands. The WCM issues severe weather warnings for the region. It is up to the WCM to explain warnings accurately so no one will be confused and respond in the wrong way. The WCM knows the towns and cities in the region and knows how severe weather will affect different groups of people.

The journey forecaster (JF) monitors radar images showing precipitation in severe weather systems. This person is trained to estimate the intensity of the storm, direction of movement, and potential for tornadoes or other damaging weather.

The hydrometeorological technician (HMT) is responsible for plotting weather data for the region. Most information is updated hourly. The HMT works closely with the JF and the WCM to locate areas where especially severe weather is likely to occur. This person also makes sure the three-dimensional model of the severe weather event is clear and shows as many aspects of the storm as possible. The job of weather-radio announcer (WRA) is usually shared by everyone in a forecast office, but for this module it will be the responsibility of the HMT unless the HMT is absent. If it is your turn to be the WRA, you will tape-record short informational messages to report weather conditions in towns around your region and announce watches and warnings when they are needed. This announcement is broadcast on National Oceanic and Atmospheric Administration (NOAA) Weather Radio and is updated every few hours, or sooner when conditions are changing rapidly.

Job Descriptions

Lead Forecaster (LF)

1. Plan and build a three-dimensional weather display.
2. Supervise analysis of hourly weather data and the development of short-range forecasts and warnings.
3. Review and approve warnings before they are issued to the public; communicate with adjacent weather stations.
4. Keep a journal with all data, forecasts, and warnings issued during the task.
5. After the severe weather passes, assemble the evaluations of your team's performances and prepare a memo to NOAA Headquarters.

Science and Operations Officer (SOO)

1. Make a cross-sectional diagram of a thunderstorm.
2. Prepare a brief explanation of air currents and changes in the physical state of water within a cloud.
3. Assist the LF in designing a three-dimensional display.

4. Assist the HMT in plotting and analyzing data.
5. Evaluate your own performance during the severe weather event. Write a paragraph about your performance for the memo to headquarters.

Warnings-Coordination Meteorologist (WCM)

1. Make a map of the region served by your forecast office. Show roads, train tracks, towns, cities, and bodies of water. Laminate the map if possible.
2. Write the statements warning of severe weather when needed.
3. Produce a pamphlet telling what people should do during a severe weather warning. Your pamphlet can be for any one of these audiences: school staff and students, drivers, athletes, people who work outdoors, airport authorities, or homeowners.
4. Evaluate your own performance during the severe weather event. Write a paragraph about your performance for the memo to headquarters.

Journey Forecaster (JF)

1. Color code radar images. Analyze them to locate severe storms in your region.
2. Calculate the speed and direction of the severe storms.
3. Estimate each storm's rainfall potential and severity.
4. Make a poster display of the radar image showing when the most severe weather occurred.
5. Assist the SOO as requested.
6. Evaluate your own performance during the severe weather event. Write a paragraph about your performance for the memo to headquarters.

Hydrometeorological Technician (HMT)

1. Plot and analyze weather data. Share your analysis with the members of your forecast office.
2. Compare your analysis with that of the JF.
3. Assist the WCM with the map and pamphlet.
4. Serve as the weather radio announcer.
   a. Make an audiotape of a simulated broadcast for NOAA Weather Radio.
   b. Assist the LF in the construction of Task products.
5. Evaluate your own performance during the severe weather event. Write a paragraph about your performance for the memo to headquarters.

STUDENT VOICES

It was scary. The tornado went over our house. I was glad it didn't touch down on us. I looked outside one time and saw things flying—papers, leaves, and stuff. I just stayed in my room and sat on the bed listening to the radio. One of my teachers got hurt. My friends at school and I talked about how bad the tornado had been on people.

STACEY PARKER
PIEDMONT, ALABAMA

Discovery File

Tornado Tool Kit

How do you stay informed about storms that might produce tornadoes? Commercial radio and television stations provide important information. But the best way to receive warnings directly from the National Weather Service is by NOAA Weather Radio. NOAA stands for the National Oceanic and Atmospheric Administration.

The National Weather Service continually broadcasts updated weather forecasts and warnings through the NOAA Weather Radio Network. This network comprises about 380 stations across the United States. About 90 percent of the nation is within listening range of a NOAA Weather Radio broadcast.

When conditions are right for severe weather to develop, a severe thunderstorm or tornado *watch* is issued by the Weather Service. Using weather radar, ground spotters, and other sources, the service will broadcast severe thunderstorm and tornado *warnings* for areas where severe weather is imminent.

Watches and warnings can be directly received by NOAA weather radios. These radios are sold in many electronics and hobby stores. The average range of the radio is 40 miles, depending on the landscape. The best of these radios are those that can be plugged in and have battery backup. The best also have a tone-alert feature that automatically alerts you when a watch or warning is issued.

Discovery File

Squall-Line Thunderstorms

Squall lines are lines of thunderstorms that can stretch for 250 miles. They form a weather system. This means they are organized: various parts of the storm have a relationship with other parts.

Squall lines develop in the middle latitudes. In North America, they occur across the United States east of the Rockies. They are also found in the tropics. Middle-latitude squall lines yield strong, straight-line winds, hail, and sometimes tornadoes.

Squall lines can form along a cold front (a mass of cold air pushing through warm air). More commonly, they develop about 160 kilometers (100 miles) ahead of an advancing cold front. The air at that point tends to be warm and moist. The actual cause of squall lines that appear well in advance of cold fronts is still under investigation.

The Supercell: The King of Thunderstorms

When conditions are just right, a supercell can develop. A supercell will develop either by itself or on the southwestern end of a squall line. A normal thunderstorm might last 40 minutes, but a supercell can last several hours. Traveling 200 miles or more per hour, a supercell often throws out a series of strong tornadoes.

A supercell is created by a unique and complicated mixture of atmospheric forces. The length and power of the supercell is controlled by how the winds flow around the central updraft. Then the supercell flows downward at the back edge of the storm to create a downdraft.

The organization of the supercell keeps a flow of warm, humid air moving into the storm. This air-flow pattern powers the storm for hours. Additional power is added to supercell and squall-line thunderstorms when rain quickly evaporates into dry air.

DISCOVERY FILE

Tornado-Watching Technology

How do you keep an eye on bad weather? To forecast and track a tornado, a wide array of technology is put to use. Satellites, radar, communications systems, automated detection hardware, and super-speed computers—all of these are very important.

The National Oceanic and Atmospheric Administration (NOAA) runs the National Weather Service. One of the Weather Service's jobs is to provide timely and precise severe weather and flood warnings.

Presently, NOAA is modernizing the National Weather Service. This means they are upgrading the service's use of advanced technology. For instance, the Next Generation Weather Radar, called NEXRAD for short, is being built. NEXRAD radars will allow forecasters to "see" inside storms and detect wind-driven precipitation. NEXRAD can spot such things as wind rotation, which can lead to a tornado.

NEXRAD makes use of Doppler radar. This weather radar can detect air movement toward or away from the radar. Doppler radar detects strong rotation within a storm. This rotation is shown on Doppler radar screens when red and green are side-by-side on the radar screen. Red on the radar screen indicates winds moving away from the radar. Green means winds are blowing toward the radar. Where these opposite direction winds touch, the swirl of a tornado is likely. NEXRAD automatically scans the sky from near the surface of the earth to the top of the atmosphere.

From a viewpoint in space, NOAA satellites also keep a day-and-night vigil on weather happenings. A new generation of Geostationary Operational Environmental Satellites (GOES) is being orbited. Positioned at various spots above the earth, GOES can track large-scale weather features. Sensors aboard GOES can detect weather patterns and chart temperatures. Infrared sensors can map temperatures in storm systems, even at night. GOES can zoom in on a significant weather event every five minutes while continuing to provide an overall view of the earth.

The National Weather Service is also installing the Automated Surface Observing System (ASOS) at many U.S. airports. ASOS operates around the clock, alerting forecasters and pilots of major weather changes. ASOS instruments gather data about such things as cloud cover, temperature, atmospheric pressure, precipitation, and wind speed and direction. This information flows directly to National Weather Service Offices and local airport control towers. ASOS data are also broadcast to pilots via a computer-generated voice.

High-speed computers are being used to link all National Weather Service centers and field offices. Weather data are also made available to the news media, which then relay the information to the public. Scientists are also using computers to model severe weather conditions.

From radar and computer networks to high-flying satellites and high-speed computers, new technology and new science combine to provide nationwide weather prediction.

IN THE NEWS

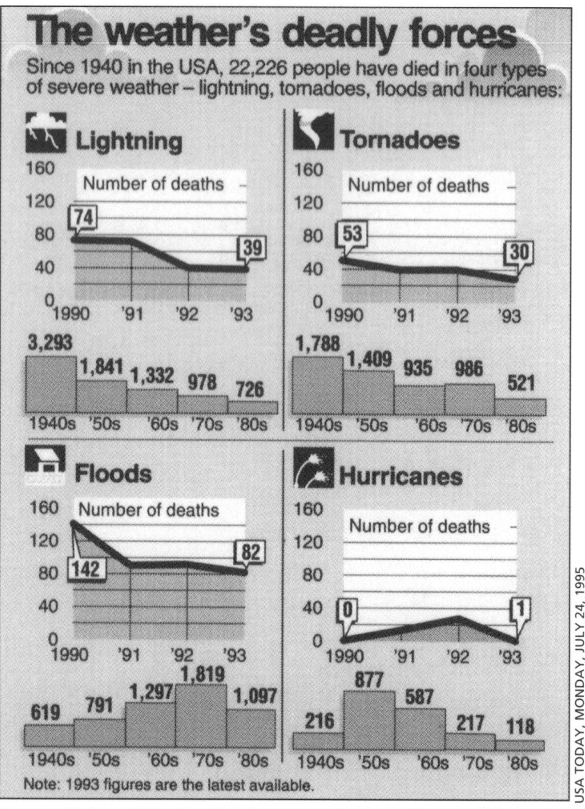

Source: National Weather Service By Kevin Rechin, USA Today

DISCOVERY FILE

Auntie Em! It's a Tornado!

A tornado is a violently rotating column of air extending from a thunderstorm to the ground. Thunderstorms develop in warm, moist air at the front edges of cold, eastward-moving air masses. They often produce hail and strong winds as well as tornadoes.

Tornadoes, with their wind speeds of 400 kilometers (250 miles) per hour or more, can cause tremendous destruction. Their damage paths can be in excess of 1 1/2 kilometers (1 mile) wide and 80 kilometers (50 miles) long. One tornado in Broken Bow, Oklahoma, carried a motel sign 30 miles and dropped it in Arkansas. Meteorologists use the Fujita tornado-intensity scale to gauge the damage caused by a tornado and to estimate the twister's wind speed. (See the Discovery File "How Intense" on page 37.)

PHOTO: THOMAS P. GRAZULIS, THE TORNADO PROJECT

Where and When Do Tornadoes Occur?

The United States is the land of twisters. Most of the world's tornadoes occur here. Tornadoes sometimes occur in other parts of the world. Tornadoes are even thought to occur on Mars. The Martian atmosphere experiences massive seasonal dust storms.

Every year, about a 1,000 tornadoes touch down in the United States. They result in an average of 80 deaths and more than 1,500 injuries yearly. Though tornadoes can hit any time of year, they are more frequent in April, May, and June. They tend to occur most often between four and six o'clock in the afternoon.

How Do Tornadoes Form?

Before tornadoes develop, a change in wind direction and an increase in wind speed, with increasing height, creates an invisible, horizontal spinning effect in the lower atmosphere.

Rising air within a thunderstorm's updraft tilts the rotating air from horizontal to vertical. An area of rotation, 3 to 10 kilometers (2 to 6 miles) wide, now extends through much of the storm. Most strong and violent tornadoes form within this area of strong rotation.

Some tornadoes form during the early stages of rapidly developing thunderstorms. This type of tornado is most common along the front range of the Rocky Mountains, the Plains, and the western states. Tornadoes may appear nearly transparent until dust and debris are picked up. If they pick up red soil, they will appear red.

As a tornado moves from a cloud downward toward the ground, it makes a hissing sound. When the twister touches down, the hiss is replaced by a deafening roar.

Occasionally, two or more tornadoes occur at the same time. One type of this tornado system is called a multiple-vortex (funnel-shaped cloud) tornado. Several funnels form and rotate within the parent cloud.

Tornadoes and Hurricanes

When hurricanes hit land, tornadoes sometimes form within the hurricane itself. But compared to the other damage from the hurricane, their effects are minor. Hurricane-spawned tornadoes are usually found in the right front quadrant of the hurricane. Winds are usually less than 160 kilometers (100 miles) per hour.

Science and Operations Officer

PETE BROWNING
NATIONAL WEATHER SERVICE
PLEASANT HILL, MISSOURI

My oldest brother got me involved in monitoring the weather when I was in fourth grade. He bought some weather instruments at a hobby store for about $20, and put them up in our backyard. We had an anemometer for measuring wind speed, a rain gauge, and a temperature sensor. We started keeping track of the daily temperatures. Since then, I have been very interested in science and weather. I was thinking about being a meteorologist at an early age.

My high-school counselor helped me select the courses I needed. Subjects such as chemistry, physics, and mathematics prepared me for college. Of course, earth science was valuable too.

I was interested in a career in weather because I was fascinated by the clouds. I liked the changing nature of the weather and the unpredictability of it. When I got to college, I found out that before we even started to study meteorology, we had to study math. Calculus, differential equations, and university-level physics—that was the hard part. The math was a challenge, but it was necessary background for understanding meteorology. You just have to stick with it.

Today computers play a big role in weather forecasting. Doppler radar, automated sur-

face instruments, and radio-broadcast equipment are technologies we use every day. A general knowledge of computers is a necessity, but you receive specialized training once you are working with the National Weather Service.

My job as a science and operations officer is to integrate recently proven meteorology research into our day-to-day weather forecasting. In doing this, we try to provide better weather forecasts for the people of northwest Missouri and eastern Kansas.

So as a part of my job, I give training seminars. I work one-on-one with the forecasters while they are doing their job. I help them to use new technologies or to think about new ideas in their daily operations.

Sometimes there are local effects to learn more about. So another part of my job is developing or overseeing research on our local weather. I also spend some of my time at the forecast desk.

A good example of how our weather-monitoring technology has improved occurred during an intense storm—the Andover event. A thunderstorm was detected early by Doppler radar in Oklahoma City. The storm was moving out of northern Oklahoma. With the old radar, we would have known there was a thunderstorm, but we would not have known what was going on inside it. With Doppler radar, we could see the severe tornado risk. We were able to issue a tornado warning. We are already seeing dramatic improvements in our abilities to forecast with new technologies.

As computer technology continues to evolve, we will be able to run more detailed computer models of the physics of the atmosphere. That should give us better two- or three-day forecasts and maybe better long-term outlooks, too.

Here is some advice for your task of monitoring and predicting severe weather conditions. When you are analyzing weather charts, look for areas where low-level convergence could occur. That is where the wind barbs are pointed at each other. Thunderstorms form along boundaries, especially frontal boundaries, in the atmosphere.

Also look for areas where you see changes in the moisture and temperature and where the winds are sort of pointing toward each other. Analyze dew points and look at the moisture field. Look for tight gradients of temperature and moisture. That will help you find the boundaries. It will be along one of these boundaries where you'll find the thunderstorms that produce the tornadoes.

SCIENCE ACTIVITY

RADAR Spelled Backward Is . . .

Purpose

To interpret weather radar images using a radarscope simulator.

Background

Meteorologists like to observe approaching weather. The sooner they see a weather system coming, the better their forecasts can be. But on stormy and overcast days, nearby clouds often block the view of approaching weather. Even on clear days, there is a limit to how far one can see.

Weather radar is a tool that makes it possible to see weather from far away. Weather radar can show precipitation inside of a cloud. Meteorologists also use weather radar to watch the sky for developing or approaching severe weather situations.

Droplets that form clouds are too small to be seen by radar. But the drops and particles big enough to fall as rain, snow, sleet, and hail are visible. Trained meteorologists watch their radar screens, looking for patterns that indicate severe weather.

The Association of University Women in your community group wants to learn more about how radar is used to predict severe weather. Their president has asked you and your partner to come to their meeting next week and speak about weather radar. You have decided to build a small radar simulator. You plan to take these simulators with you so group members can better understand the art of forecasting during a rapidly changing storm situation.

Radarscope Simulator

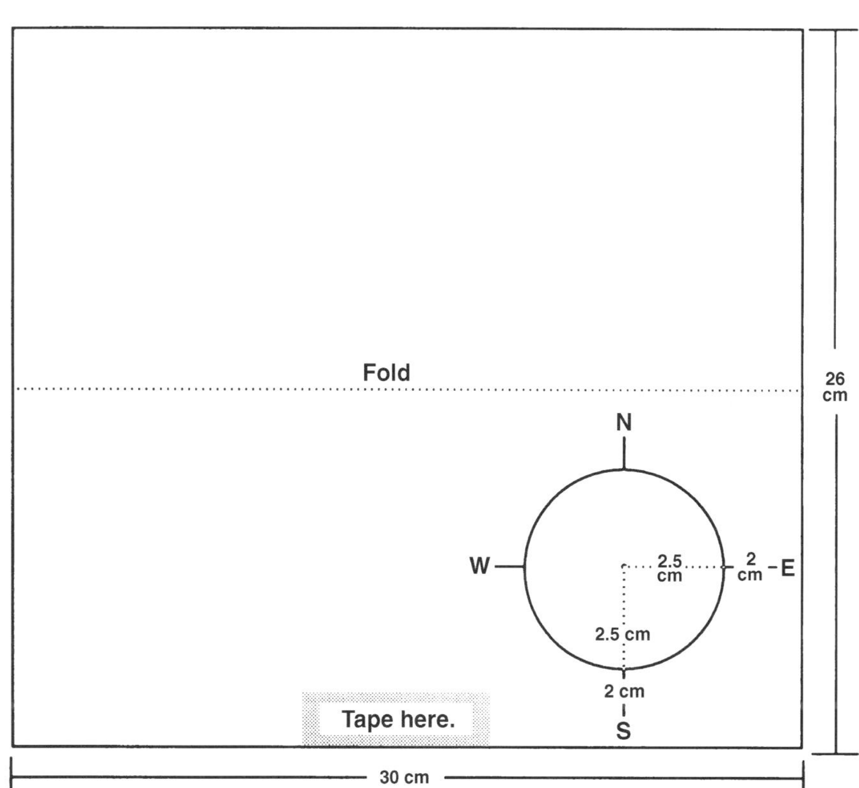

Materials

For each pair:

- Heavy paperboard (posterboard, tagboard, or file folder)
- Tape
- Transparency plastic (clear acetate)
- Ruler
- Colored pencils or crayons in the following colors: light green, dark green, yellow, orange, and red
- Drawing compass
- Scissors
- Stapler
- Nonpermanent transparency marker
- Permanent marker
- Sample sequence of radar views (from the teacher)
- Videotape player/recorder (optional)

Procedure

1. Cut a 26-by-30-centimeter rectangle from the posterboard. Draw a 5-centimeter-diameter circle near one corner of the posterboard, as shown in the diagram above. The circle should be on the right-hand side of the folded board. Carefully cut out the circle to make a window.
2. Mark north, south, east, and west around the window as shown. Cut a piece of transparency plastic and tape it to the inside of the window.

➤ continued on page 20

➤ continued from page 19

Fold the board as shown by the dashed line, and tape it closed along the long edge to make the radar-scope simulator.

3. Neatly draw a distance scale beside the window, showing that 6 millimeters equals 20 kilometers.
4. Your teacher will now give you a strip of paper with three radar scenes on it for you to use. Color these radar scenes, starting with the outside band and coloring it light green. Move to the next band inside and color it dark green. Follow the color chart below. As you move in the radar scene, you move up the chart.
5. Now slide the strip with its colored scenes into the simulator. Make sure it slides freely and that one scene at a time is visible through the window.
6. Adjust the radar scenes so the 3:00 P.M. scene is centered in the window. Using a permanent marker, make a small dot on the window at the center of the display.
7. The speed of a storm is the distance it moves divided by the time it takes to move that distance (kilometers per hour or km/hr). Brainstorm with your group methods you can use to find the speed of each thunderstorm as it moves across the radar screen. You may write on the transparent material using a nonpermanent marker.

Radar Scene Color Chart

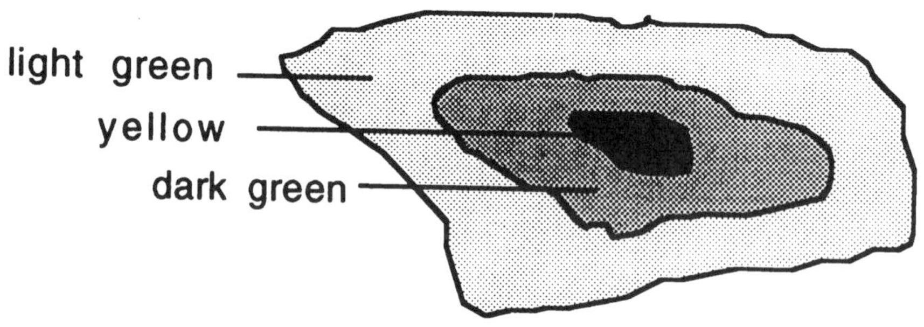

Conclusion

1. Notice that the radar echo near your station does not move. What could be producing that echo?
2. The president of the community group called. This is the message that was left:

> *Please send me an outline of your presentation. You will have about ten minutes to explain how you read weather radar and forecast rainfall amounts. I'll see you next week.*

   Prepare the outline, indicating the approximate time you will spend talking about each item in your outline. Be sure to explain how the colors are used.

3. If you have the equipment at home, videotape part of a local television weather report showing weather radar for your community or videotape a segment from The Weather Channel. How will you use this tape in your presentation?

Color Chart for Interpreting Weather Radar Images

Intensity	Description Code	Color	Rainfall (est. per hour)	Comments
6	Extremely Severe	Red	More than 7.1"	Includes large severe hail, damaging winds
5	Intensely Severe	Red-Orange	4.5"–7.1"	Includes hail as well as rain, wind, and lightning
4	Severe	Orange	2.2"–4.5"	Very heavy rain and lightning
3	Heavy	Yellow	1.1"–2.2"	Heavy rain and lightning
2	Moderate	Dark Green	0.2"–1.1"	Some lightning
1	Light	Light Green	Less than 0.2"	

Use the above chart to make forecasts for thunderstorm cells shown in the radar-scope simulator. (Use this information during the Task, too. It will help you make forecasts for the communities surrounding your station.)

Grief, wonder in Alabama town

Survivors grappling with 'void'

By Paul Hoversten
USA TODAY

PIEDMONT, Ala. — By all rights, Ricky Shadrix should have been sitting in a pew Sunday morning at Goshen United Methodist Church.

But, in a decision that may have saved his life, Shadrix instead drove to Montgomery to visit a friend in prison.

"It's the only time I've been glad to go to a jail," said Shadrix, 36, who joined the church just a week before. "You could say I was lucky."

But Shadrix, like so many in this tight-knit town of 5,500, didn't escape untouched by the tornado that destroyed the church Sunday, killing 23 people and injuring 92.

As flags flew at half-staff in a drizzling rain Monday, Shadrix and others mourned their losses and marveled at what survived after storms swept across the South last weekend, killing at least 43 in Alabama, Georgia, Tennessee and the Carolinas.

The storm system that spawned about 30 tornadoes in four states moved northeast Monday, producing heavy rain and flood warnings from North Carolina to Connecticut.

"There's enough rain that's occurred in general, and more coming in, that's probably going to put some areas over the edge," said Jim Carbone of Weather Services Corp.

In Piedmont, Shadrix was stunned to learn that his employer at a gas and convenience store, Earl Abbott, 54, died inside the church, along with Abbott's 5-year-old grandson, John.

"Earl was like a father to me," said Shadrix, sadly. "And John, he was a sweet kid."

Others told similar tales of a how the twister ripped through a town where relatives, friends and neighbors are intertwined.

Piedmont, at the foot of the Appalachian Mountains, lies in a stretch of east Alabama known as "Tornado Alley." About 100 years ago, a twister killed more than 40 people.

But no one was prepared for the disaster that struck Sunday. As the horror sunk in, residents rallied around the minister of Goshen United, Kelly Clem, whose 4-year-old daughter, Hannah, died at the church.

Monday, Clem walked through the church's wreckage with her husband, Dale, clutching a stuffed pink cat that belonged to her daughter.

Clem, whose face was battered and gashed by flying bricks, said that after the storm she prayed with church members who kept asking "Why, Kelly? Tell me why?"

Clem said she told them: "We do not know why. I don't think 'why' is the question right now. We just have to help each other through it."

As news of the disaster spread, donations poured in Monday. At a "command post" at Piedmont's civic center, the outpouring was so heavy that officials told callers to bring only non-perishable goods, diapers and baby formula.

Many in town, like Doris Curtis, were preparing for funerals later this week. When the tornado hit, Curtis lost two cousins, Cicero and Ti Peak, who came from their nursing home to attend church Sunday.

"Piedmont's going to pick itself up, but there will always be a void," Curtis said. "This is something the town will never really get over."

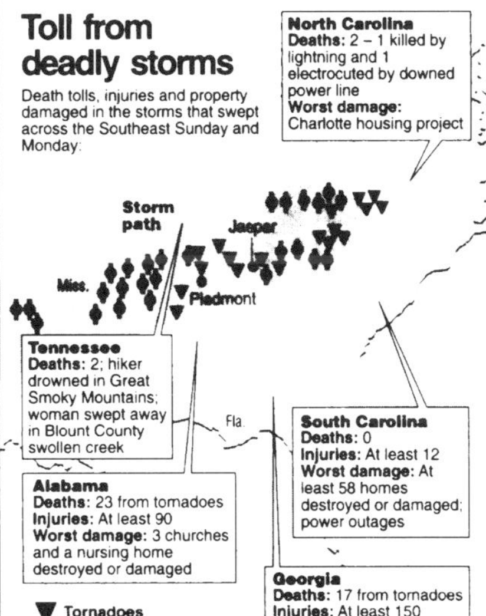

Source: Weather Services Corp., AP — By Marty Baumann, USA TODAY

Photos by Dave Martin, AP

TRAGIC LOSS: The Rev. Kelly Clem clutches a stuffed pink cat that belonged to daughter Hannah, who was killed Sunday. With Clem: Bishop Robert Fannin, left, and the Rev. Herb Williamson.

When warnings came, it was already too late

By Mimi Hall
and Jack Williams
USA TODAY

If only Alabama's Calhoun County had been able to install the warning sirens officials had requested.

If only the tornado warning had been broadcast on the radio an hour earlier.

The tragedy that struck Piedmont Sunday might have been avoided with a combination of high-tech tracking, human spotters, emergency broadcasts and sirens.

But timing was a tragic factor. And earlier warnings couldn't be issued because weather experts say tornadoes are the hardest kind of dangerous weather to predict.

New, sensitive weather radars being installed around the country detect early signs of tornadoes — but even they can give only up to 30 minutes' warning.

It wasn't until 11:02 a.m. Sunday that the National Weather Service issued a formal tornado warning for the vicinity of Piedmont.

By then, it was too late. Scores of worshipers were inside Goshen United, and Palm Sunday services were in progress.

At that point, only sirens could have helped. Alabama's big cities have warning sirens, and Calhoun County recently installed them in nearby Anniston, because of a potentially dangerous chemical weapons stockpile.

Alabama officials asked the federal government for money to install sirens across the rest of the Calhoun County, including Piedmont. But the request was denied.

And in cases when even high-tech radar systems don't predict tornadoes, experts say people trained to spot tornadoes could help with earlier warnings.

Says Steven Cooper of the National Weather Service: "We'll always need those trained eyes to give us truth on what's going on."

USA TODAY, TUESDAY, MARCH 29, 1994

THE STORY—PART 2

Route of Ruin

The destruction of the Goshen United Methodist Church was just one saga produced by tornadoes in the southeastern United States. On that same day, numerous tornadoes sliced across north-central Alabama and northern Georgia and then ripped into the Carolinas.

They twisted their way over the four-state landscape. A trail of devastation was left behind—43 deaths, 320 injuries, and more than $105 million in property damaged. Alabama was hardest hit with 23 fatalities. Georgia lost 18 people. Two deaths occurred in North Carolina. More than 350 residences were destroyed and nearly 850 residences were damaged throughout the three states.

Oddly, the large-scale weather features that usually spawn an outbreak of tornadoes were missing. However, as early as Saturday, March 26, 1994, weather forecasters had begun to see an ominous trend.

They noticed small-scale weather patterns with dangerous potential. They knew these small-scale disturbances could whip up tornadoes. Weather watchers at the National Severe Storms Forecast Center (NSSFC) in Kansas City monitored the telltale signs. They saw air-mass instability, strong wind-shear patterns, and a lot of moisture over the south-eastern United States.

STUDENT VOICES

I lost a friend from school in the tornado. That has taught me how to appreciate everything I have and everybody I love to be with. Now when I study bad things at school, I think about what the people might be going through. I pray for them, and I hope they are better in the end. I am thankful that I am not going through anything like that.

PATRICK JOHNSON
PIEDMONT, ALABAMA

When warm, moist air meets cool, dry air, the mix can trigger severe thunderstorms and tornadoes. It became apparent trouble was brewing!

The NSSFC began to issue public severe weather outlooks and watches. There was talk of possible tornadoes and severe thunderstorms. At 2 A.M. on March 26, the NSSFC issued a "threat of tornadoes" watch. The storms, if they were going to form, would follow a pattern. One local meteorologist later called it a "tornado alley." This tornado alley stretched from St. Clair through Calhoun and Etowah counties up to Cherokee.

Waves of tornado-producing thunderstorms called *supercells* began moving across a narrow band of countryside in the southeastern United States. These supercells produced as many as 18 tornadoes that touched down in Alabama and Georgia. Two separate supercells that spawned tornadoes moved across several counties in a northeasterly direction at speeds up to 65 miles per hour. Weather surveillance was mostly carried out by radar.

The tornado that passed so near to the Goshen church in southern Cherokee County had its origins from a severe thunderstorm that formed in eastern Jefferson County, Alabama. As it moved eastward into St. Clair County, the storm strengthened into a supercell. At 10:55 A.M. on March 27, a half-mile-wide tornado emerged from the supercell on the southeast side of a town called Ragland.

As the tornado moved across the most easterly part of St. Clair County to H. Neeley Henry Lake, it claimed its first life. Several boaters in Ten Islands Historic Park saw the approaching storm clouds. They raced back to a boat ramp at the park. The tornado sailed across the boat ramp at 11:05 A.M. Its powerful force flipped boats high into the air. The pile of upturned boats crushed one person and seriously injured another.

The tornado crossed H. Neeley Henry Lake and continued its rampage. Another person was killed as the tornado struck a vehicle moving along on a highway northwest of Piedmont.

Over the next hour, the tornado hit the Goshen church and continued northeast, hammering rural portions of Cherokee County. The tornado then weakened and evaporated in northwestern Polk Country, Georgia. By that time, it had crossed 200 miles from its origin in Ragland in east-central Alabama.

The tornado's lethal route of ruin left hundreds of people mourning the deaths of family members and friends. The townspeople began to sift through demolished homes. They inspected damaged farmland and surveyed destroyed businesses.

Alabama

IN THE NEWS

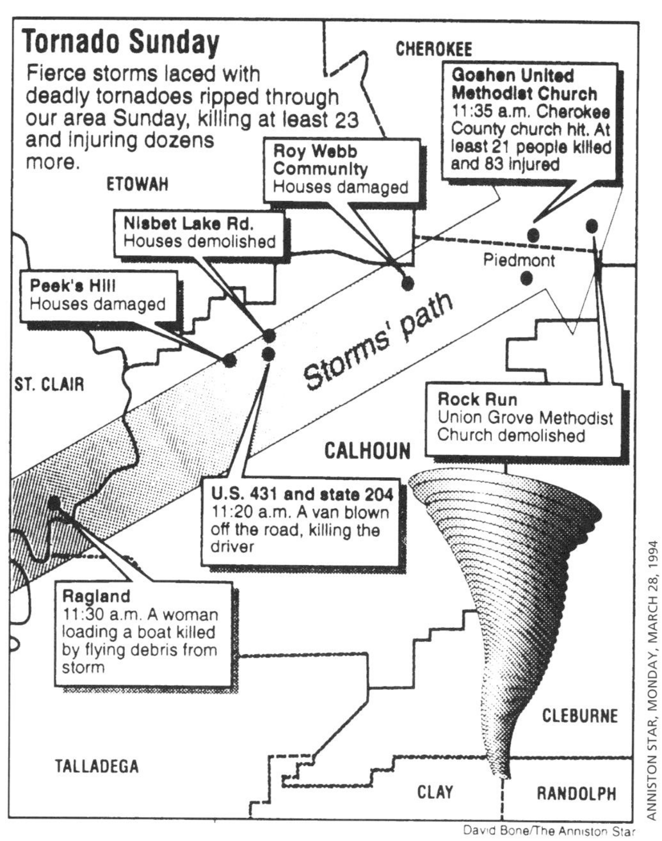

David Bone/The Anniston Star

ANNISTON STAR, MONDAY, MARCH 28, 1994

Discovery File

Reading a Weather Map: Highs, Lows, and Fronts

Constructing a weather map that accurately forecasts weather across the United States takes a cast of thousands. Meteorologists need millions of observations from weather stations, weather ships, satellites, balloons, and radar. Every minute, these instruments are taking detailed readings of temperature, pressure, wind direction, and other relevant measurements.

The data they gather are entered into the Global Telecommunications System (GTS). GTS relays data to powerful supercomputers that assemble a picture of atmospheric conditions around the world. From these maps, the computers are able to create forecasts up to seven days in advance.

Newspaper weather maps are easy to understand if you know the definitions of a few meteorological terms and what the symbols represent.

Highs and Lows

Areas of high- and low-atmospheric (air) pressure are represented by an *H* or *L* in the center of a black circle. Lines that join points with the same air pressure are called *isobars.* Newspaper weather maps usually do not show isobars; instead they often show *isotherms.* Isotherms are lines that connect points with the same temperature.

Pressure systems "drive" the world's weather, so forecasting the weather is dependent upon locating ridges of high pressure and troughs of low pressure.

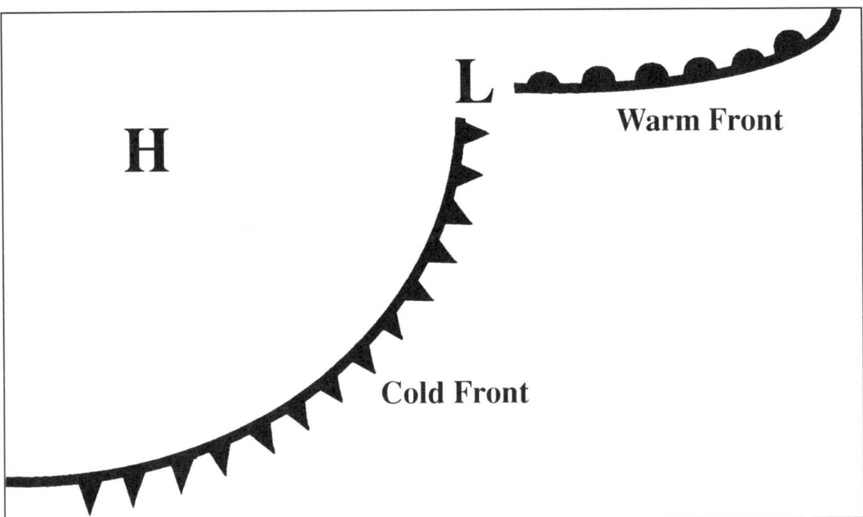

Fronts

The air around us is constantly being either warmed or cooled by the surfaces over which it travels. At any given time, there are large masses of the atmosphere that are either warm or cold. When these warm and cold air masses bump into each other, a boundary called a *front* is formed. When the warm air is pushing through, the boundary is called a *warm front.* A *cold front* indicates the cold air mass is pushing its way through. A standoff between the two air masses is called a *stationary front.*

It is along these fronts that dramatic and sometimes violent weather occurs. The mixing of cold and warm air causes clouds to form along the front and produce rain. Fronts often travel very fast. When a cold front passes through your town, a thunderstorm might quickly be followed by a sunny day. The effect of a warm front lasts longer. As it approaches, clouds slowly increase. Then the rain begins and lasts for several hours.

Cold fronts are usually indicated on a weather map as lines with triangles pointing out from the line. The symbol for warm fronts is a line with semicircles dotting it. Stationary fronts have alternating triangles and semicircles.

Dry Fronts

A *dry front* or *dry line* is another area where thunderstorms frequently develop. Dry fronts occur mostly during the spring in the Central Plains. Dry fronts separate very warm, moist air to the east from hot, dry air to the west. As a dry front moves east during the afternoon hours, tornado-producing thunderstorms may form.

DISCOVERY FILE

Weather-Station Symbols

The diagram at the bottom of the page is a sample of a station code. A station code is a way mete- orologists plot a lot of information on a small map. The following summarizes what each symbol means.

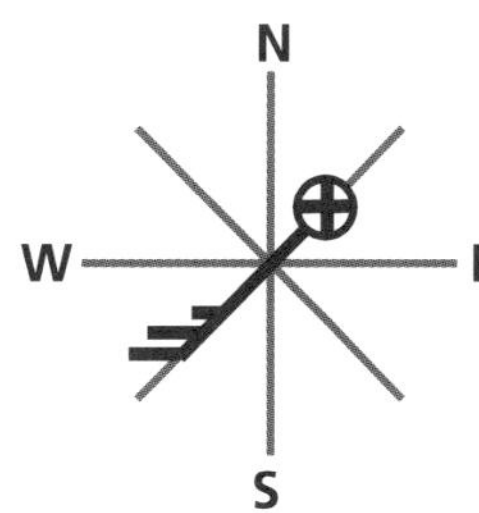

The flagstaff shows the direction from which the wind is blowing. This shows the wind blowing toward the northeast. The flags show the windspeed.

- about 1 knot
- about 5 knots
- about 10 knots
- about 50 knots
- So this means the wind is blowing at about 25 knots

Because space is limited on a weather map, barometric pressure is plotted using only the last three digits. The first number is either a 10 or a 9. Notice in the diagram that the measurement of 125 really means 1012.5 millibars. The 10 is understood, and the decimal is omitted.

For example, 990.5 mb becomes 905 when it is put in a diagram. You will rarely find a barometric pressure reading below 950.0 mb or above 1050.0 mb (both of which would read 500). So if you see 655 on the map, it is much more likely to mean 965.5 mb than 1065.5 mb.

The sky condition and current weather also appear on the symbol. Here are some of the symbols used.

Sky Condition

- clear
- scattered clouds
- partly cloudy
- broken clouds
- overcast
- sky obscured

Current Weather

- rain
- sleet
- drizzle
- haze
- thunderstorm
- rain shower
- snow
- freezing rain
- fog
- smoke
- hailstorm
- snow flurry

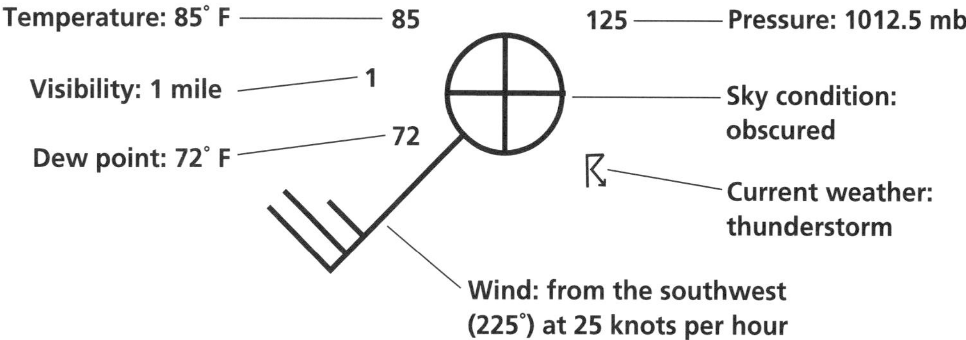

DISCOVERY FILE

Tornado Alley

"Tornado Alley" is the name given to the narrow band of land where most tornadoes develop in the United States. Tornado Alley crosses four states—Kansas, Missouri, Oklahoma, and Texas. If you live in Tornado Alley or in another state where tornadoes are common, your school probably has tornado drills in addition to fire drills.

Most of the world's tornadoes form in the midwestern United States. During the spring and early summer, conditions there are perfect for these violent storms to form. The greatest number of U.S. tornadoes (about 75 percent) occur between March and July. April tornadoes have caused the largest number of deaths.

Tornadoes are destructive to both people and property, yet people live in Tornado Alley. Why do people risk their lives to live there?

Decisions in life often involve balancing risks and benefits. For example, farmers are attracted to rich soil. If that rich soil is on the side of a volcano, farmers gamble that the volcano will not erupt during their lifetimes.

Farmers on the plains and in the midwestern corn belt choose to live in the paths of tornadoes. The soil is good, and the same conditions that produce tornadoes and severe storms also bring 80 percent of the rain during the growing season. Water can be a big expense for a large farm, so having it fall from the sky for free is a benefit that needs to be weighed heavily against the unpredictable risks of severe weather.

IN THE NEWS

Aftermath: Touring the ruins

Survivors search ruins, arrange funeral services

By Richard Coe
Star Staff Writer

SPRING GARDEN — Foster Freeman is set to retire Wednesday from his job at SCT Yarns Inc. But he won't stop working.

Freeman, like hundreds of others in northeast Alabama, is homeless. The house in Cherokee County that he called home for 12 years was destroyed Sunday when tornadoes ripped through the region. The only room left standing was the bathroom, where he and his wife hid during the storm.

"I'm just trying to get everything up, find a place to put it, and see if I'm going to try to rebuild," he said Monday as he rummaged through his destroyed home for belongings.

Freeman is not alone. All over the region, homeowners spent Monday and today scavenging through debris, looking for scraps of their lives. They are among the more fortunate: other families spent the day making arrangements to bury their dead.

Emergency officials, meanwhile, continue to tally the damage from the Palm Sunday storm: 22 dead, 156 injured, hundreds more homeless. Estimates of the dollar amount of damage will take several more days to compile.

Sunday focused on removing bodies and saving the survivors trapped beneath the wreckage of Goshen United Methodist Church, where 20 people died when a wall and roof collapsed during a Palm Sunday service. The first funeral for a church victim was today; a number of others are scheduled Wednesday.

To help the victims of Sunday's storm, see story/9A.

ON MONDAY, Cherokee County EMA Director Leon Smith toured the rest of the destruction in a white van sheathed in winking strobes. He counted 52 homes destroyed, 32 with major damage, 21 with minor damage. The bellowing winds also destroyed two other churches in the county: the Pleasant Valley Church and the Union Grove Baptist Church.

"It seemed like mobile homes just exploded," Smith said. "They were just in pieces."

Delois Champ, spokeswoman for Calhoun County EMA, said 75 homes and barns in Calhoun County were destroyed. Another 13 homes suffered major damage and 40 were slightly damaged.

She said EMA teams were out on the road again today to assess damage to public property, such as roads, bridges and utilities.

Jesse Culp, a spokesman for Cherokee Electric Cooperative, which serves Cherokee County and northern Calhoun County, said he still had several hundred homes without power this morning.

All along Cherokee County Road 4, debris from people's homes splotched the grassy hills Monday. Tin from chicken houses was wrapped around utility polls like ribbon.

UP THE ROAD from Freeman, residents hauled mattresses and cots into Spring Garden High School for the homeless. Kaye Kaufmann, a Huntsville Red Cross worker assigned to the storm area, said it will be offering free food to storm victims.

"Most people don't have any clothes or houses anymore," said Courtney Colvard from behind the counter at her family's general store on U.S. 278. "A lot of people up here lost family in the church in Goshen. This was awful."

Help is expected to come from the

■ See Survivors/9A

Rev. Kelly Clem tours her damaged church

By Jenny Cromie
Star Staff Writer

GOSHEN — The Rev. Kelly Clem lost her house and lost her church. She lost 20 members of her congregation and she lost her 4-year-old daughter, Hannah.

But the pastor's faith was unshaken by the tornado that ripped through the Goshen United Methodist Church.

Clutching the pink stuffed cat Hannah got for Christmas, Rev. Clem returned Monday morning to her church, where 24 hours earlier a tornado tragically halted the Palm Sunday service she was leading, altering her life and the lives of her congregation forever.

Her left eye bruised and swollen shut, Rev. Clem walked deliberately around the site with area United Methodist clergy and her husband, assessing the loss and retrieving a few personal belongings from her parsonage next to the church.

Slowly, she walked over to the entrance of the sanctuary, cordoned off by a yellow ribbon, and into her office. Out of the rubble-filled church she came a few minutes later, gripping a gold mirror her mother had made. Somehow, it was unshattered.

However small, it was one thing still intact.

"I'm holding up," she said, somehow mustering a smile. "People are holding me up."

■ See Clem/10A

ANNISTON STAR, TUESDAY, MARCH 29, 1994

IN THE NEWS

Tornados slam Oklahoma; toll in Texas hits 18

By Steve Marshall
and Sandra Sanchez
USA TODAY

Tornados in Oklahoma killed at least three people Sunday, while in Texas, the death toll from bad weather hit 18.

The Oklahoma deaths were in a small farming community near Marietta, police dispatcher Kenny Walker said. Three women were hurt. A tornado also hit Ardmore, about 20 miles north on Interstate 35.

Texas officials continued searching for three men believed killed in storms that injured at least 100. Damage was set at $400 million.

The Ardmore tornado damaged a Circuit City warehouse that was under construction and a tire plant. No one was seriously injured, officials said.

"We had some warning before the tornado, and that's probably what saved a lot of lives," said Joe Elles, emergency management director in the city of 23,000.

One school and 30 houses were damaged and five houses destroyed, Elles said.

Twisted metal dangled from upper reaches of the Uniroyal building, where several hundred employees were at work.

"We understand everyone was in a shelter," said Jim Morton, a spokesman for Uniroyal-Goodrich in Greenville, S.C.

Dana Baird, a former television news reporter, said she was traveling with her family in a car to Dallas when the rain became so heavy on Interstate 35 that they had to pull over.

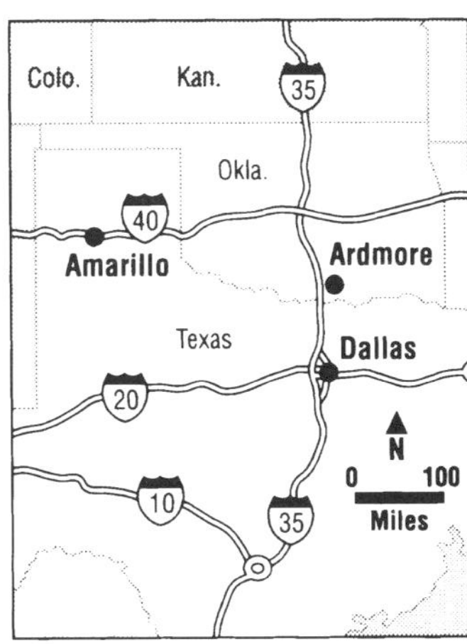

USA TODAY

When the rain let up, they saw the damage: "Twisted metal all over the place," she said.

In Texas, the storm death toll rose to 18 after a tornado blasted the Amarillo area Sunday, killing one man and leaving five people seriously hurt.

Robert LeGrand, 38, was killed when the tornado smashed his mobile home.

LeGrand's body was found 130 feet from where he had stood on his front porch.

In Dallas, rescuers searched for three people pulled down a manhole bv 10-foot floodwaters Friday night.

Missing were two motorists trapped by rising water and a man who tried to help them, said Carolyn Garcia, a spokeswoman for the city's office of emergency preparedness.

A whirlpool sucked all three into a tunnel that drains into the Trinity River.

Since the storms hit Friday, 13 people have drowned, two died in lightning-related accidents and two were killed when a warehouse roof collapsed. The tornado killed one.

The first string of storms brought winds of 70 mph and dropped softball-sized hail on Mayfest celebrators in Forth Worth on Friday night, then swept motorists away with flash floods in Dallas.

And in Clovis, N.M., a tornado Saturday uprooted telephone poles, overturned mobile homes and sent shards of glass flying around the southeastern part of town, but police say no one was killed or seriously injured.

The severe weather was spawned by a system that began developing last Thursday, said meteorologist Vinny Moise of Weather Services Corp. "It's just a big whirling storm out there that keeps bringing severe weather," he said. "And it's just not moving."

But, Moise said, there may be good weather news ahead: "We're expecting some movement of the storm in the next day or so, and that should alleviate the severity."

USA TODAY, MAY 8, 1995

Discovery File

Weather Hazards for Aircraft

It is not easy to keep an aircraft safe. Hurricanes, volcanic-ash clouds, and birds must be avoided. In addition, weather experts must alert pilots when downbursts, wind shear, and wing icing pose a threat.

Downburst and Microburst

Downbursts and microbursts were discovered in the 1970s. Theodore Fujita (the scientist who invented the tornado damage scale) was surveying storm damage from the air. He noticed that some tree damage was in what he called a *starburst pattern.* It was different from the circular or semicircular-circular destruction left by tornadoes.

Fujita's research led to the detection of *downbursts.* He defined a downburst as any wind blasting downward from a thunderstorm. *Microbursts* are the most dangerous kind. They can encompass an area less than 4 kilometers (2.5 miles) across. Their winds can exceed 240 kilometers (150 miles) per hour.

The threat to airplanes is especially serious during a plane's landing approach to an airport. If a plane encounters a strong headwind of a microburst, its nose will tend to rise and the airspeed will climb rapidly. A pilot's natural reaction in this situation is to push the plane's nose down and throttle back the engines. This combination, however, can lead to disaster. When the plane leaves the microburst, the wind shifts. What was a strong headwind becomes an equally strong tailwind. The pilot's actions, which were correct for a headwind, turn into a disaster in a tailwind. The plane stalls, goes into a dive, and crashes.

Wind Shear

Wind shear is often associated with a downburst. It has been thought to be the cause of a number of airline crashes. Wind shear refers to a quick change in wind speed or direction. It can be found at high altitudes in the jet stream, near the ground, or anywhere in between. Wind shear can be vertical or horizontal.

When you experience turbulence in an airplane, it is because of wind shear. You are flying through an area where the wind's speed or direction changes rapidly. The difference in wind speeds stirs up eddies, or whirlwinds, that cause a bumpy ride.

Winds blowing past each other in different directions also produce wind shear. This type of wind shear is found near the ground when warm winds are blowing over cold, calm air.

A wind-speed change of more than 16 kilometers (10 miles) per hour in a 30-meter (100-foot) distance is considered a strong wind shear. A change of more than 23 kilometers (14 miles) per hour in 30 meters (100 feet) is a severe wind shear.

Wing Icing

Pilots have an additional fear—wing icing. Aircraft accidents caused by icing have claimed the lives of about 40 people a year since the 1970s. Icing is especially dangerous for single-engine or small twin-engine aircraft, including commuter airplanes. In late 1994, pilots even protested the safety of some commuter planes they were asked to fly. First pilots refused to take them up in icy weather; then the Federal Aviation Agency (FAA) ordered the grounding of ATRs (a small commuter plane especially prone to ice buildup).

What is wing icing? When supercooled water drops (in freezing rain or in a cloud) hit an airplane, they freeze instantly. Ice collects on wings and increases air resistance. That causes drag and slows the plane down. It also changes the shape of the wings. A combination of slowing and shape change reduces the lifting force that keeps a plane airborne. Ice also adds weight. To reduce the hazards of wind ice, planes are treated with wing-deicing chemicals right before they take off.

IN THE NEWS

FAA grounds planes in icy weather

'This is going to put a lot of people on the road. . . . Inherently it's far safer to fly'

By Kevin Johnson and Paul Hoversten
USA TODAY

CHICAGO — Dan Ballegeer, tired and unshaven after a tough weekend of job hunting in Dallas, was bewildered.

He had arrived at O'Hare International Airport Sunday to find his American Eagle flight — on an ATR aircraft — back to the University of Illinois in Champagne had been canceled.

So like hundreds of other travelers stranded nationwide he could take a bus, fly to Indianapolis to catch a connecting flight or rent a car.

"I guess I'd rather drive than crash," he says.

Ballegeer isn't the only one taking the wheel after the Federal Aviation Administration ordered the ATR grounded in icy conditions. About 15% of all seats on regional carriers will be affected as airlines scramble to replace the French-Italian built ATRs with aircraft deemed less hazardous in wintry weather.

"There's still going to be disruptions," says David Stempler of the International Airline Passengers Association. "You can't pull that much capacity out of the system without having some disruptions."

The association advised its 110,000 members not to fly the planes after the Halloween crash of an American Eagle ATR-72 that killed 68. Ice buildup is suspected as the cause.

"It's going to scramble the (aviation) equation very bad-

Please see COVER STORY next page ▶

IN THE NEWS

Hurt 'Girl' gets a lift

By Ric Feld, AP

CANINE VICTIM: Jan Brown, left, and Tim Yongue carry his dog Girl from his tornado-wrecked, Piedmont, Ala., home Monday. The twister killed at least 44 people. **(Warnings too late, 3A)**

USA TODAY, TUESDAY, MARCH 29, 1994

ON THE JOB

Journey Forecaster/Radar Meteorologist

TOM BRADSHAW
NATIONAL WEATHER SERVICE
BIRMINGHAM, ALABAMA

I grew up in Oklahoma. Most people in that part of the country are very aware of the weather because it changes so much. And the weather in Oklahoma can be quite severe at times. Living there, you get used to the tornado sirens going off. Sometimes tornado outbreaks happen two or three times in the spring. Head for the shelter!

I'm called a journeyman forecaster. Forecasters work around the clock, with two forecasters on each shift. One is a lead forecaster and the other is a journeyman, usually someone younger. I'm the younger one.

My interest in weather began quite early. I was always interested in earth science, astronomy, geology, and meteorology as a young person. In fact, I was always looking at the sky and chasing thunderstorms. So I fell into a career path at an early age.

I got my bachelor's degree from the University of Oklahoma. They have a very good meteorology program. I got my masters degree at Florida State University. Doing research or being a television weatherperson wasn't for me. I joined the National Weather Service as an intern. Just a few years ago, I became a forecaster.

Working for the federal government is the best career path I could have taken. The federal government is probably the largest employer of meteorologists.

I have to admit the toughest challenge for me was math. There is quite a bit of math in this work, and math was not one of my strengths. But I worked hard and overcame that problem.

If you're interested in meteorology, it helps if you are math-oriented, but being a hard worker is just as good. Take a science or math track in junior high or high school. That will help you in the long run. Courses in chemistry, physics, and computers are important, too.

My work involves a number of computers. The National Weather Service is probably one of the most computer-intensive organizations in the federal government. We use computers constantly. Some of our computers are tied to a radar system. Many of our computers are part of a network. We are able to exchange data across the country.

A new piece of hardware that we have just started to use is the NEXRAD. That stands for Next Generation Weather Radar. It is a critical tool in watching for severe weather patterns.

A typical day involves the issuing of forecasts. There are two types of forecasts we issue daily. One type is for the general public. The other forecast is for the aviation community—from small to medium-sized airports. Making forecast advisories for the aviation community is what I do.

I start my eight-hour shift by looking at all the weather data that has come in. I look at the latest weather-satellite data and radar information. In two and a half hours, I issue ten forecasts. Once those go out, I amend them as the weather evolves.

You never know what might pop up unexpectedly. Things can get hectic. If you have a line of thunderstorms moving through your area, you may be putting out four or five warnings at a time.

My job is very satisfying. Weather changes constantly, and that makes my job far from dull. When you see a place that has been hit by a tornado, the power of nature really comes home to you.

It is satisfying to see that the information you put out is of immediate help to people.

Watching the weatherperson on television give out the information I have provided is quite rewarding. Once in a while, we will get someone complaining to us that it rained on his or her picnic. But we receive far more compliments than complaints.

When you are studying weather charts and gathering information, you are like a weather detective. Search for clues. Where are storms likely to form and why?

For instance, if a cold front is moving through Kansas, storms are probably going to form along that cold front. Why? Well, because that is where the wind and the moisture come together. They are converging and only have one place to go—up! Typically, rising unstable air is the spot where a storm forms. That is the place to keep your eye on.

Being a weather forecaster means seeing whether you can outwit Mother Nature.

IN THE NEWS

Sifting for clues, stem to stern

Investigators piece together crash mystery

By Linda Kanamine
and Gary Fields
USA TODAY

One minute before USAir Flight 1016 crashed, killing at least 37 of its 57 aboard, ground control issued a wind-shear alert warning pilots but not prohibiting them from landing. Investigators are looking at wind shear as one possible cause of the crash. How wind shear – sudden changes in wind speed or direction – can affect aircraft:

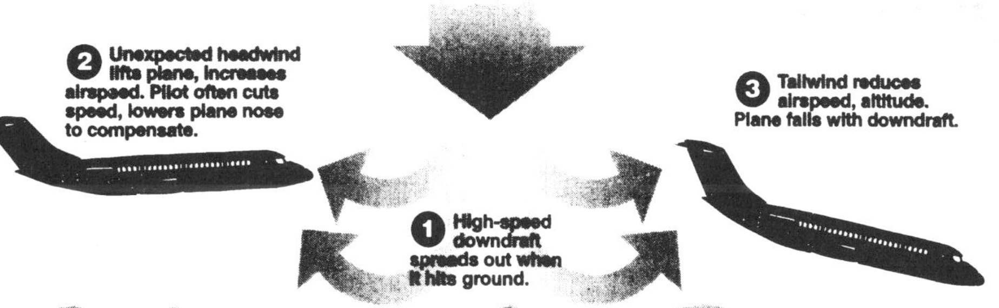

Chronology of USAir Flight 1016

1. About 6:40 p.m. Saturday, plane attempts landing during thunderstorm. Pilot radios that he is aborting landing.

2. Pilot tells tower he is "up to 3,000 (feet), we're making a right turn here." Twenty seconds later, plane dives and crashes.

3. Plane hits clearing, bounces and skids into trees, breaks into three sections. Tail crashes into house.

Old Dowd Road · Pieces · Wallace Neel Rd. · Charlotte-Douglas International Airport · CHARLOTTE · 74 · 85 · 1 · 160 · N · 0 · 1 · Mile

Ky. · Charlotte · Va. · Durham · Tenn. · Raleigh · 40 · 95 · N.C. · Ga. · S.C.

Radar still uncommon

Charlotte's airport currently uses a low-level wind-shear indicator. Airports with a more-accurate Doppler radar now:

Memphis International
Will Rogers World (Oklahoma City)
William P. Hobby (Houston)
Hartsfield-Atlanta International
Washington National
Denver International
Chicago O'Hare International
Lambert St. Louis International
Orlando International
New Orleans International (not active)

Sources: Federal Aviation Administration; USA TODAY research

By Stephen Conley, USA TODAY

CHARLOTTE, N.C. — Disaster detectives combing the strewn wreckage of USAir Flight 1016 are dissecting every clue — from the tail section imbedded in a house to cables and cockpit gauges.

Today, investigators question the crew for details of what happened in the moments before 6:40 p.m. Saturday, when the DC-9 flight from Columbia, S.C., crashed during a thunderstorm. Thirty-seven of the 52 passengers died; all five crew members survived.

At least one person on the ground was hurt. No one was in the house that was hit.

"It's a jigsaw puzzle the investigators slowly put back together," says National Transportation Safety Board spokesman Alan Pollock.

Gruesome, tedious sifting through charred, twisted metal began within hours of the crash. But a solution to this mystery will take months.

Among the leading suspects is weather, particularly wind shear that often comes with severe thunderstorms, like those buffeting Charlotte Saturday.

"The rain and scud was so heavy that runway 1-8 right was obscured," the NTSB's John Hammerschmidt said late Monday after interviews with the tower controllers. The "controller never saw the aircraft ... until the controller saw smoke coming from the crash site."

Charlotte-Douglas International Airport issued a wind-shear warning a minute before the crash and the pilots discussed "strategy," he says.

Wind shear presents one of the greatest hazards during takeoffs and landings, when large gusts of wind can suddenly slam down on planes.

The FAA several years ago launched pilot training programs — which Flight 1016 Capt. Michael Greenlee and First Officer James Hayes reportedly took.

The FAA is installing Doppler radar, which detects wind shear, at busy U.S. airports that suffer severe weather. Ten cities have it; Charlotte gets the $2.5 million system in 1995.

Still, flight decisions ultimately rest with pilots.

A USAir flight that landed 2½ minutes before Flight 1016 told NTSB agents it encountered light rain upon landing, but hit heavy rain while it was slowing down on the runway.

Investigators also are reviewing control tower tapes and interviewing crews of other planes that delayed takeoff. What they'll look at:

▶ Life stories of the USAir crew members, their training, and activities in the 72 hours before the crash.

▶ Stories of survivors like Army air traffic controller Stanley Williams and his wife. "The wind was playing havoc with the aircraft. I felt the power to the engines and saw the rudders were down," says Williams, who suffered burns. "By the time the jet dropped out of the clouds we were 200 feet above the ground, but the plane was at a 45-degree angle to the runway. ... He did a good job getting the nose up. If he hadn't, there wouldn't have been any survivors."

▶ Flight recorder boxes with cockpit conversations.

▶ Maintenance records for the plane, in service since 1973.

In the field where the plane skidded 1,100 feet before breaking into three parts, investigators scrambled to collect evidence as rain threatened. Every piece is important: The filament in lightbulbs from cockpit switches, for instance, can show if instruments were on or off during the crash.

The scene has drawn hundreds of onlookers like Verida Curry, 42, who came "to give my prayers to the lost ones. It makes me wonder what they were thinking. It's a funny thing to know you're going to die and you don't have a chance to say anything."

Contributing: Erin Einhorn and Margaret Litvin

USA TODAY, JULY 5, 1994

SCIENCE ACTIVITY

Make the Code, Break the Code!

Purpose

To use the weather-station code to find a cold front; to construct a map of surface observations using weather-station code.

Background

You are the new air-traffic controller at the Topeka Airport. The time is 3:35 P.M. (central daylight time). A dangerous cold front is moving in. You have the weather map for 3:00 P.M., but it is full of symbols. What do they mean? You also have data for 4:00 P.M. observations, but you don't have a map. You pick up the phone to call the local forecast office for help, but a storm has knocked out the phones! You must find the cold front on the map so you can advise pilots. Should they take off or stay on the ground?

But wait! A page in an old notebook has a key to the symbols. You can use the key to break the code and locate the cold front.

Materials

For each group:

- Discovery File "Weather Station Symbols" (page 26)
- Surface Observations 3:00 P.M. (from the teacher)

For each student:

- List of narrative weather observations (from Appendix)
- Blank map (from the teacher)

Procedure

1. Use this module and other references to learn as much as you can about weather fronts. Study the Discovery File "Weather Station Symbols" on page 26.
2. From your teacher, get the surface observations from 3:00 P.M. Find the cold front on this map. Hint: Look for stations near each other that have very different weather conditions.
3. Get the blank map from your teacher. Use the data in the Appendix for the weather observations for 4:00 P.M. (central daylight time). Put the data on the blank map using correct station code symbols for the stations listed.
4. Examine the map carefully and draw a line across the map representing the cold front.

Conclusion

1. Using your map as a guide, decide whether or not you will allow pilots to take off. Explain your answer.
2. Between 3:00 P.M. and 4:00 P.M., where was the front going? Does this information change the status of the airport?

Storm Shelters

The Palm Sunday tornado outbreak of 1994 wreaked havoc on people and property.

Storm victims also included animals. One twister left about 20,000 hens sitting in steel cages within the wreckage of their hen house. Many hens were plucked of their feathers and perched atop broken eggs and dead chickens. Cows wandered aimlessly in open pastures. Family cats roamed the area looking for home or had to be rescued from trees. At a 200-acre park that contained 150 animals, kangaroos appeared to be in shock. A deer and an African wildebeest were found dead.

Property damage was widespread. One woman described the tornado as "a freight train in stereo." She jumped into a bedroom closet as the tornado narrowly missed her house. The tornadoes blew cars and trucks hundreds of yards. They flattened campers and trailers after tossing them into the air. They lifted some houses from their foundations and tore the roofs off others. One tornado battered a nursing home. Utility poles were snapped like twigs, leaving more than 75,000 Alabama residents without power for several days.

The tornadoes also overturned historical landmarks. Oak, pine, and dogwood trees were uprooted or broken in two. Some trees were bent over, with roots showing above ground as their branches lay across damaged cars and houses.

STUDENT VOICES

We all got into a closed space in our bathroom. There were four of us: my mother, my dad, my sister, and me. When my dad went outside, he saw a big black cloud coming over the house. "Get back in the bathroom," he yelled. I heard the tornado. It sounded like a train.

SHARI CANTRELL
PIEDMONT, ALABAMA

Tornado winds were ferocious. For example, the wind carried a canceled check 130 miles away from its owner's destroyed mobile home in Piedmont.

The center of the tornado that leveled the Goshen United Methodist Church contained winds rated on the Fujita scale at F3—between 158 and 206 miles per hour. The Fujita scale is used to gauge the intensity of a tornado. The Goshen tornado actually passed about 200 yards north of the church, not striking the actual building. The southern side of the tornado broadsided the south roof and wall of the church. Estimates of the wind speeds that pounded the structure were placed at F1 on the Fujita scale—73 to 112 miles per hour. Investigators estimated that residences surrounding the church were damaged by wind speeds of about 100 miles per hour.

Whipping through the area, the tornado center passed north of the church. But the steep angle of the church's roof and the height of its walls acted as a sail to catch the wind. The roof and walls collapsed as the winds twisted them to the north. Debris from the roof and wall fell into the church and onto the congregation.

Investigators of the tornado-hit church observed that an interior hallway remained intact. All those in the church could have found shelter in the hallway.

As with other tornado events in the United States, the majority of those killed in the four-state sweep of destruction were in mobile homes. Single and double-wide mobile homes provide little shelter from tornado effects because they are not anchored to a floor or foundation. Mobile-home residents do not have a basement or any other quick access to shelter when a tornado strikes.

Many people whose homes were ravaged by tornadoes survived without serious injury. They had moved to their basements or storm shelters. Others who outlived the ordeal sought shelter in crawl spaces, bathrooms, or center hallways. Those who were spared injury or death avoided rooms and buildings with large roof spans.

Sadly, the loss of life at the Goshen church, and at various other locations, provided important lessons that should not be soon forgotten.

IN THE NEWS

Ala. town 'pulls together'

As funeral services begin, help pours in

By Paul Hoversten
USA TODAY

PIEDMONT, Ala. — A grieving town began the grim task of burying its dead Tuesday, still searching for answers amid a tornado's bewildering devestation.

"We're here today with heavy hearts full of grief, full of pain," the Rev. Leeann Scarbrough told mourners at services for Ethelene Blair.

"We'll continue to ask 'Why?' for a long, long time. And we'll continue to hurt for a long time. But I know comfort will come."

Blair, a 54-year-old supervisor at a textile plant, was among 20 people who died when a tornado stuck Goshen United Methodist Church during Palm Sunday services. More than 90 people also were injured, part of a storm that swept across four Southern states, killing 44 people.

More funerals will be held in Piedmont throughout the week, including services for Hannah Clem, 4-year-old daughter of the Rev. Kelly Clem, who is minister at Goshen.

Since the Goshen sanctuary was destroyed, Blair's funeral was held at First Presbyterian Church Tuesday.

That same afternoon, George Scroggin came to take one last look at the building where his father, George Sr., and brother, Kirk, had died. Then he drove on to their funerals in nearby Centre.

"We've heard from so many people and that's what got us through all this. It's amazing how much people cared," said Scroggin, 45, who was in the church when the tornado hit.

"I had my cry and now I'm here to support other people if I can. We'll get my dad and brother buried and then see what we can do to help others," he said.

Scroggin vowed the church would regroup: "We've had offers from other churches to join up. We'll find a way as a church to get together."

There were signs Tuesday of a town on the mend.

By Dave Martin, AP

OVERCOME: Kevin Siersma wipes his eyes Tuesday amid the tornado-torn rubble of Goshen United Methodist Church in Piedmont, Ala. Siersma's cousin, 4-year-old Hannah Clem, was one of six children killed.

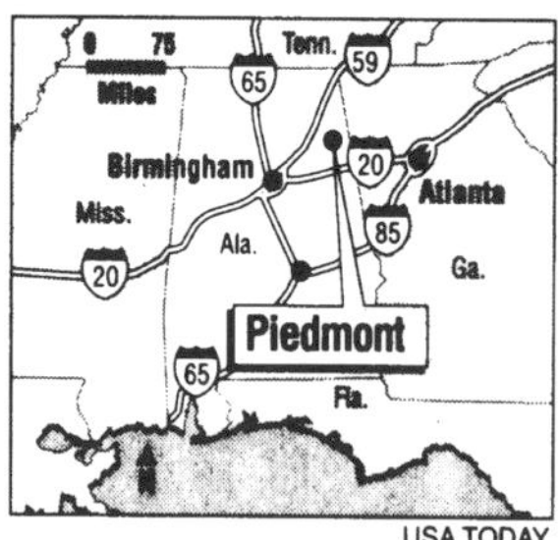

USA TODAY

At the town's civic center, volunteers were piling up donated food, clothes, diapers, soap and other goods. Calls kept pouring in to say more was on the way: a truckload of furniture from a company in Tupelo, Miss.; 20 mattresses from another in Jasper, Ala.

"Everybody keeps pulling together and helping one another," said C.E. Curtis, 60, a retired aluminum worker, who will attend two funerals today.

"But everyone's lost someone so you don't know who to turn to because they've had losses of their own."

Said city Councilman Bill Baker: "The shock's still there but people are starting to move forward and do what they need to do to rebuild their lives."

The tornado is now in the record books as Alabama's sixth worst storm.

Statewide, Alabama emergency management officials say they need federal aid totaling $12.5 million to help individuals and businesses, and another $7.5 million to repair public facilities and remove debris. The state will provide $3.9 million.

Officials counted 383 homes or trailers destroyed and another 1,069 damaged.

Vice President Gore and Agriculture Secretary Mike Espy are scheduled inspect the damage today. Alabama Gov. Jim Folsom and Democratic Sen. Howell Heflin toured the area Tuesday.

As members of the Goshen church sifted through debris, lifting out a Bible stand and collection plates, Clem told Folsom there were no tornado sirens in the area and no one knew a twister was on the way Sunday.

"If we had known there was a warning, we would not have met," said Clem. "Maybe you can do something about that."

USA TODAY, MARCH 30, 1994

DISCOVERY FILE

Tornado Safety

Tornadoes can develop so quickly that warnings are often impossible. Is there anything you can do to increase your safety? By planning ahead, you will not lose your head when critical moments could mean possible injury or worse.

First of all, develop a plan for yourself and your family before a tornado threatens. You should have plans for times when you're at home, work, school, or outdoors. Be familiar with the names of surrounding towns, counties, and roads. Weather bulletins often name a storm's current position and direction of movement.

An important tornado safety tool is a NOAA (National Oceanic and Atmospheric Administration) weather radio. A good weather radio should have a warning-alarm tone and battery backup. It is designed to receive warnings when severe weather threatens. It is also important to keep your eyes and ears tuned to the radio and television for weather-related information. If you are planning a trip outdoors, listen to the latest forecasts and plan accordingly if threatening weather is possible.

What do you do when a warning is issued? Move quickly to an underground shelter, such as a basement. If an underground shelter is not available, move to an interior room or hallway on the lowest floor and get under a sturdy piece of furniture. Stay away from windows!

If you are in an automobile, get out. Do not try to outrun a tornado in your car. Outside your vehicle, lie flat in a nearby ditch or depression. Do not forget that if you are in a mobile home—even if it's tied down—you have little protection against a tornado. Abandon the mobile home and get to a safer place.

Remember, being safe from tornadoes means being prepared.

DISCOVERY FILE

Thunderstorm Tips and Lightning Lessons

Here are a few safety tips to learn before a storm rumbles your way. Know the county in which you live and the names of nearby major cities. Severe weather warnings are issued on a county basis. If you're going to be outside for an extended period of time, check the weather forecast. Always keep an eye out for approaching storms. If a storm is approaching, stay tuned to an AM/FM radio or a radio designed to receive weather reports.

If you hear thunder, you are close enough to get struck by lightning. Go to a safe shelter immediately. Move to a sturdy building. Do not seek shelter in small sheds or under isolated trees. If you are in a boat, get to shore and away from the water as fast as you can.

If you are caught outdoors with no shelter nearby, make yourself the smallest target possible. You can do that by squatting low to the ground on the balls of your feet. Then put your hands on your knees and place your head between your knees. If you are in the woods, take shelter under the shorter trees.

If you're at home, do not take a bath or shower when thunderstorms approach. Turn off air conditioners, as power surges from lightning can overload the compressors. Telephone lines and metal pipes can conduct electricity. Unplug appliances you do not need for obtaining weather information. Use phones only in an emergency. If you are using your computer, save your work frequently, or better yet, unplug the computer until the storm passes.

In the event that a storm causes loss of heat, power, and telephone service, a few precautions are worth taking. Keep flashlights and extra batteries available. Have a first-aid kit on hand and restock any missing items. Consider emergency heating sources and have a fire extinguisher and smoke detector nearby that work.

ON THE JOB

Hydrometeorological Technician

LEO RITTER
NATIONAL WEATHER SERVICE
WICHITA, KANSAS

Meteorology is an extremely challenging field, but you never get into a rut or a routine. One day it's sunny, the next day it's rainy—there is constant change. I have been in the weather business for about 40 years, and I still enjoy every day.

I am a hydrometeorological technician (HMT) in Wichita, Kansas. My job does not require a four-year college degree. I started my career in meteorology while I was in the military. I didn't ask for a position in weather, but my test scores were high, which led the military to place me in their weather-service branch.

Military weather work meant a lot of travel around the world. It was a very prestigious field to be in. After the military, I went to work for the National Weather Service (NWS).

Though it wasn't required for my job, I went back to school and took the courses to qualify as a meteorologist. I now supervise the hydrometeorological technicians at our NWS office.

On a typical day when we walk into work, we get a change-of-shift briefing. We find out how the weather may look during our shift. Also, we learn whether any equipment is having problems. We use a checklist, checking the radar and other equipment.

At the top of each hour, we prepare a weather broadcast. Current weather information is broadcast over the NOAA Weather Radio System. NOAA is the branch of the U.S. government that administers the National Weather Service. We have a radio room at our forecasting center to broadcast our reports to several surrounding counties.

In my field, there is quite a lot of specialized training. For instance, I had to take a 16-week course on observing. I was taught to evaluate sky conditions, estimate cloud heights, read various instruments, and do the required calculations.

Over the years, there has been a continuing evolution of equipment; the technology is always changing. I remember when transmitting one weather map took 18 minutes. Now all transmitting is computerized and takes only seconds. We are always upgrading and adding new weather-monitoring devices. This requires continuous learning, too.

If you are interested in meteorology, I have a few recommendations. First, take all the math you possibly can. If you can get algebra in eighth grade, more power to you. If you can study calculus in high school, it will help you get ready for college math.

In addition to math and science classes, take a typing class. Typing will teach you to use a keyboard—very important for operating weather-monitoring computers. Also try to take as many computer classes as possible.

High-school students might want to volunteer to work with someone who is involved with our cooperative weather-observer program. Farmers, storekeepers, police, and others call in their weather and climatological observations. They provide rainfall data and temperature measurements. They call us immediately if they sight a tornado.

We work around the clock. Twenty-four hours a day, there are people at the more than 200 National Weather Service Forecasting Centers across the country. We work eight-hour shifts: 8:00 A.M. to 4:00 P.M., 4:00 P.M. to midnight, or midnight to 8:00 A.M. That is one of the drawbacks of the weather business. The weather never rests. It has to be monitored all the time.

As you work on the task in this module, remember that weather can change very quickly. You and your team should try to stay on top of things. Try to notice these changes early. If you start noticing very high dew points (a measure of moisture) coming in, that could be a sign that a frontal system is moving into the area. If wind speeds increase too, you have the makings of severe weather. That frontal boundary causes the moist air to rise and makes the air mass very unstable.

When this happens, not only is the atmosphere outside changing, but the atmosphere inside the weather station is changing, too. You can feel the static electricity of excitement in the station. Usually there are just a few of us per shift. But when severe weather is coming, we get extra help immediately. Phone calls increase. The pace of getting the severe weather advisories out to the public quickens. Our weather station can become quite a frantic place to be.

DISCOVERY FILE

How Intense

Tornadoes are classified on the Fujita tornado intensity scale. Fujita categories link the extent of damage to a tornado's wind speed.

Category	Definition/Effect
F0	Gale tornado (40–72 mph): Light damage. Damages some chimneys and sign boards; breaks branches off trees; pushes over shallow-rooted trees.
F1	Moderate tornado (73–112 mph): Moderate damage. Lower limit (73 mph) is the beginning of hurricane wind speed. Peels surface off roofs; pushes mobile homes off foundations or overturns them; pushes moving autos off roads.
F2	Significant tornado (113–157 mph): Considerable damage. Tears roofs off frame houses; demolishes mobile homes; pushes over boxcars; snaps or uproots large trees; generates light-object missiles.
F3	Severe tornado (158–206 mph): Severe damage. Tears roofs and some walls off well-constructed houses; overturns trains; uproots most trees; lifts heavy cars off ground and throws them.
F4	Devastating tornado (207–260 mph): Devastating damage. Levels well-constructed houses; blows structures with weak foundations some distance; throws cars; generates large missiles.
F5	Incredible tornado (261–318 mph): Incredible damage. Lifts strong frame houses off foundations and carries them considerable distances until disintegrated; sends automobile-sized missiles through the air in excess of 100 yards; debarks trees; creates other incredible phenomena.

DISCOVERY FILE

Flashers and Boomers: Lightning and Thunder

Lightning can be awesome, but sometimes it's fatal. It is estimated that lightning strikes the earth about 100 times every second. Lightning is one of the most common weather phenomena. Although lightning strikes often, it is still not completely understood.

Some cultures believe lightning gives healing powers to those it hits. In at least one case, the strike itself seemed to heal. Edwin Robinson of Falmouth, Maine, who was blind for nine years, was hit by lightning in 1980. When he came to, he reportedly could see.

Lightning results from the buildup and discharge of electrical energy. It occurs between positively and negatively charged areas. These areas may be in different parts of the same cloud, between different clouds, or between a cloud and the earth.

The earth develops a positive charge during a storm. The lower regions of thunderclouds carry a negative charge. Attracted by this negative energy in the low clouds, positive charges gather on the tops of buildings, trees, or other elevated objects—including people. When the attraction becomes strong enough, negatively charged electrons zigzag toward the ground. This is called the *stepped leader*. As the stepped leader nears the ground, it attracts a streamer of positive charge toward it. When the stepped leader touches the rising streamer, lightning flashes.

The lightning flash itself is a return stroke of positively charged particles racing upward toward the cloud. The return stroke travels at one-third the speed of light (about 60,000 miles per second) and can repeat several times along the same path in less than half a second.

The air near a lightning strike is heated to 50,000 degrees Fahrenheit. That is hotter than the surface of the sun! The rapid heating and cooling of air near the lightning causes a shock wave that produces the sound we call thunder. A bolt of lightning can pack up to 100 million volts of electricity.

Different sounds of thunder come from different parts of a lightning bolt. The loudest crash comes from the main trunk of a bolt. The sharper crackling sounds come from the branches.

To estimate the distance in kilometers between you and the lightning flash, count the seconds between the lightning and the thunder and divide by three. (For the distance in miles, divide by five.)

Most lightning deaths occur in the summer months, during the afternoon and early evening. An average of 93 deaths and 300 injuries are blamed on lightning each year. You can reduce your risk of injury by following the lightning safety rules found in the Discovery File on page 35.

Many fires in the western United States and Alaska are started by lightning. In the past decade, more than 15,000 lightning-induced fires nationwide have resulted in several hundred million dollars a year in damage and the loss of 2 million acres of forest.

Several theories on the origin of life suggest lightning might have been a factor in the chemical reactions that led to the creation of some of the complex molecules found in living organisms. In any case, lightning can be considered both a destructive and constructive force of nature.

IN THE NEWS

USA TODAY, SEPTEMBER 28, 1992

DISCOVERY FILE

Chasers and Spotters

Chasing tornadoes is dangerous and difficult work, but someone has to do it. Tornado chasers provide data and trained-eyewitness accounts that will help us understand the science behind these swirling masses of bad weather.

Tornado-chasing scientists from the National Severe Storms Laboratory in Norman, Oklahoma, take field trips to study tornadoes. They watch storms as part of VORTEX, the Verification of the Origins of Rotation in Tornadoes Experiment. Equipment mounted on VORTEX vehicles is used to measure wind gusts, hard-driving rain, and hail. Camera crews in VORTEX chase cars race to spots where twisters might form. For a tornado chaser, blue skies mean a bad day!

In the past, scientists used instrumented barrels to gather tornado data, placing the barrels in places where twisters might form. Each barrel was called TOTO after Dorothy's small dog in *The Wizard of Oz.*

TOTO barrels have been replaced in recent years with pods called *turtles.* Turtles do not blow over as barrels can. Each turtle hugs the ground and weighs 55 pounds. Low-lying turtles are hurriedly spread out in a pattern on the ground as a tornado approaches. As the whirl of bad weather passes, each of the instrumented pods measures storm temperature and pressure.

Thanks to the increased use of video cameras, amateur tornado hunters are in the tornado-chasing business. They have documented how tornadoes form and create a trail of destruction. But scientists who chase tornadoes caution that running after twisters is dangerous. The behavior of funnel clouds is very unpredictable. Amateur tornado chasers can get themselves killed.

The National Weather Service has a network of trained tornado spotters across the country. These amateur weather watchers are trained to scan the sky for tornado conditions. What if they see a large cloud mass that is rotating at its base? That is an early warning signal of a tornado. The spotter then calls the local National Weather Service Office.

Gathering information about tornadoes is very important for public safety. With new technology, scientists are coming closer to unraveling the mysterious workings of these whirlwinds.

STUDENT VOICES

The tornado made my mother real nervous, because she had been in a tornado before. The weather kept getting darker and darker. The wind was blowing hard. I wasn't aware that the tornado had hit until I went outside. The sky was black and clouds were moving like they were going around the earth. I heard thunder, some ambulance sirens, and traffic. Stuff was strewn everywhere—car parts, tree limbs, paper. The yard looked messy.

APRIL LANGLEY
PIEDMONT, ALABAMA

Discovery File

Cloud Formation

Photo by Bill Mills

From the ground, clouds can look like huge piles of cotton or billowing mounds of whipped cream. But if you have ever flown through a cloud in an airplane or hiked at very high altitudes, you know that clouds are more like great areas of clammy, gray fog. This should not surprise us, because clouds, like fog, are made up of water droplets suspended in air.

Molecules of water vapor move about in the air, rising as the air grows warm. But as air rises, it eventually grows cooler. The air temperature drops about 3 degrees Celsius for every 300 meters, or 5.4 degrees Fahrenheit for every 1,000 feet of rise. This rate of falling temperature with increasing altitude is called the *Adiabatic Lapse Rate.*

As the rising air cools, condensation occurs and the tiny water droplets born of that condensation form a cloud. These tiny droplets condense onto solid particles and drift around in the atmosphere. The particles of sea salt, dust, and pollen, picked up by the wind as it blows over the earth, make perfect sites for condensation. And of course, as more water vapor rises to the condensation level, additional water droplets attach themselves to more particles. This increases the density and area of the cloud.

Why do some clouds look white and others look gray or even black? Some clouds are white because their water droplets or ice crystals are just the right size to scatter light of all wavelengths. First, understand that sunlight contains all the colors of the rainbow. Light travels as waves, each color possessing its own unique wavelength. When light of all wavelengths is scattered, the colors combine to produce white light.

Clouds can appear dark for several different reasons. They can be very dense with water droplets or very thick, so that they block the rays of sunlight. The top part of a cloud could also cast a shadow on its own base, or a cloud could be in the shadow of another cloud. Do not assume that dark clouds are always rain clouds. Thunderstorm clouds are very dark. That is because thunderstorm clouds rise to heights of eight miles or more. Their thickness prevents sunlight from passing through.

SCIENCE ACTIVITY

A Hot Dip on a Cold Day

Purpose

To demonstrate the circulation of water and air in the atmosphere.

Background

You are the manager of a ski resort in a volcanically active region. It is a beautiful place with many hot springs. You want to install a large heated outdoor spa for guests during their winter vacations. Nothing is ever as simple as it seems. When you show your plans to the county planning board, they say you need an environmental-impact statement explaining how the spa will change the surrounding area. Without that statement, they will not issue a permit. Before you can write the impact statement, you need to know more about what will happen. You have decided to develop a set of experiments to demonstrate the effect of the spa on its surroundings.

Materials

For each group:

- Large rectangular container with clear sides
- 1 aluminum pie pan
- Hot water
- 2 or more small plastic bags filled with small rocks, frozen
- 1 small candle
- Matches

Procedure

1. Place an aluminum pie pan in the bottom of a clear container. Place the pan near one end and stand a candle next to the pan.
2. Start the first experiment by quickly pouring some of the hot water into the pan and placing a bag of frozen rocks (your teacher will provide these) at the other end of the box. Now light the candle and quickly blow (or snuff) it out to produce smoke. Carefully place a lid on the clear box, being careful not to disturb the air inside. Caution: Put out the candle *before* you place the lid on the clear container! Do not leave the lid on while a candle is burning!
3. Make observations every minute and record all changes in the system until no more changes occur.
4. Continue trying different experiments as materials and time allow. With each new experiment, make one change to the original system. Before you perform a new experiment, predict what difference the change will make. Observe for differences. Was your prediction correct? Don't forget to record your predictions and observations.

Conclusion

1. Write an environmental-impact statement explaining the effect of the heated spa on the surroundings during the winter. Be sure to include an explanation based on your observations and use a labeled diagram if you think it will help.
2. Use what you have learned in this activity to explain what is happening in the situations described below.
   a. You leave a can of cold soda on the kitchen counter on a hot day. Water drops begin to collect on the outside of the can.
   b. A school bus is full of students on a winter day. Before the bus gets to school, the windows are fogged up on the inside.
   c. On a hot summer day, you open the freezer door in your kitchen. A cloud appears at the door and falls to the floor. When you close the freezer, the cloud disappears.
   d. It is early on a summer morning. You are camping in a valley. When you open your tent, you see that it is very foggy outside. But from the top of a nearby hill, it is clear and sunny.

Different Kinds of Precipitation

Fog

How many mystery and horror stories depend upon wispy fog for drama? Like a cloud on the ground, fog is created when there is little wind and humid air is cooled to its dew point. At the dew point, water vapor begins to condense into tiny droplets. Fog will burn off as the sun rises in the morning. The sun's warmth raises the temperature above the dew point, and the fog evaporates.

Rain

Clouds are formed from the water that evaporates from seas, lakes, rivers, humid land masses, and plants. Even sweaty joggers out for their daily runs contribute. Millions of tiny water droplets form a cloud when this evaporated water condenses around salt, dust, and other particles in the air.

Why does this condensation usually occur high in the sky? It is because cloud formation, just like fog formation, begins when the dew point is reached. As air rises, it expands and cools. Which do you think must rise higher before a cloud forms, dry air or moist air?

In order for rain, snow, sleet, or hail to start falling from the clouds, some of the droplets must increase in size a million times or more. In the case of warm rain clouds—clouds whose tops are warmer than 0 degrees Celsius (32 degrees Fahrenheit) —droplets may grow by bumping into each other inside the cloud. As they grow, they eventually become too heavy to remain suspended in the air, and they fall to the ground.

In cold clouds, with tops well below freezing, water vapor condenses to form ice crystals. Ice crystals grow quickly, and as they fall through the cloud, they collect other droplets and smaller crystals along the way. Eventually, these ice crystals will reach the ground as raindrops, snowflakes, or a mixture of rain, snow, or sleet.

Small raindrops make a light form of rain called *drizzle*. They measure less than .05 centimeters (.02 inches) across and can take as much as an hour or more to reach the ground. Drizzle generally falls from a layered cloud not more than 2 or 3 kilometers (a mile or two) thick. In contrast, a heavy, sudden shower of large raindrops usually falls from a cloud 14 kilometers (9 miles) or more thick.

Sleet

Drops of water falling from the sky, freezing as they plummet downward, can form sleet. Sleet is made of small drops of water that freeze into pellets of ice, usually smaller than 0.8 centimeters (0.3 inches) in diameter. Sleet is often mixed with liquid drops. The gentle rattling on windowpanes caused by sleet is often an early warning of an impending ice storm. Roads can turn into something like skating rinks—too dangerous to drive over—when covered with sleet.

Hail

When lumps of ice fall from thunderclouds, we experience hail. Golf-ball-sized hailstones are common in certain areas. In fact, the largest hailstone on record fell on September 3, 1979, in Kansas. It had a circumference of 44.5 centimeters (17.5 inches)! But hail is usually pea-sized and falls in short, intense showers called *hailstorms*.

Hailstones are formed when water droplets freeze into small ice crystals in a thundercloud. Strong air currents in the thundercloud toss the pieces of ice up and down between the cold and warmer parts of the cloud. Every time the hailstone enters a warmer area, moisture sticks to its surface. Each time the air current lifts it back into the colder part of the cloud, it freezes solid again. The hailstone gains several coats of ice as it is whisked up and down in the cloud. Finally, it grows too heavy to remain up in the cloud and falls to earth.

Snow

When billions of tiny ice crystals cluster together and fall from cold clouds, we have snow. The crystals are formed when the water vapor freezes directly onto dust particles in the atmosphere without becoming water droplets first. For this to happen, the upper atmosphere must be very cold, generally around –20 degrees Celsius (–4 degrees Fahrenheit). Snow crystals grow as more ice is deposited on them.

All snow crystals have six sides, but their shapes depend on how much moisture is in the air and how cold it is. Because these conditions vary greatly within a cloud, no two snowflakes are exactly alike. You have probably noticed how sometimes snow is large and fluffy and perfect for making snowballs, and at other times it is fine and powdery. Large, fluffy, wet snow generally falls at temperatures just around freezing because the freezing crystals stick together.

Snow takes up much more space than an equivalent mass of rain. In fact, because air occupies so much space within fallen snow, a fresh layer of cold snow may be up to 36 times as deep as the same amount of rainwater. Have you ever seen a "thunder snow"? When a thunderstorm develops during the winter, it has the features of a regular thunderstorm: torrential downpours with thunder and lightning. But instead of downpours of rain, a thunder snow drops several inches of snow in a very short period of time.

On March 7, 1984, a thunder snow in Washington, D.C., dropped a foot of snow in less than an hour and brought the city to a standstill.

Blizzard

A blizzard is a snowstorm with winds of more than 55 kilometers (35 miles) per hour. In a blizzard, falling and blowing snow reduce visibility to near zero.

DISCOVERY FILE

The Hydrological Cycle

Water molecules are constantly moving. They are always vibrating—faster when they are hot and slower when they are cold. Sometimes their vibrations cause them to move from place to place. If we were able to follow a single water molecule over the course of several days, we might see it change its state and location many times.

Let's imagine one possible path a water molecule might take—a single molecule on the surface of a lake. It absorbs energy from the sun. The energy of heat is transformed into energy of motion, causing the molecule to move about more rapidly. When it gains enough speed, the water molecule evaporates, leaving the surface of the lake to join other energetic water molecules in a gaseous state called *water vapor.*

The molecule, carried high into the atmosphere by updrafts of warmed air, begins to cool and lose energy. Energy loss results from the expansion of the air as it climbs higher and higher. When enough energy has been lost, the dew point is reached and the air becomes saturated. This molecule and others condense around a dust particle in the air, forming a droplet of water. As more drop-lets form and gather together, a visible cloud forms. This cloud becomes dense enough for precipitation to fall. Precipitation might be liquid (rain) or solid (sleet, snow, or hail).

The single molecule we have focused on, along with millions of other molecules, has become frozen as it is tossed to the top of a building thundercloud. First it falls through the cloud, only to be caught again in an updraft. It is tossed again and again from the bottom of the cloud to the top of the cloud. As it moves, more and more water molecules are added, and the hailstone grows. This hailstone lands on a sloping rooftop, just one of thousands of other raindrops and hailstones falling in a sudden spring thunderstorm.

The hailstone bounces down the roof and then falls to the warm ground below. Energy from the sun-warmed soil quickly melts the hailstone. It becomes a drop of water on the ground. Other drops join it to become a trickle. Trickles merge as they flow down a hill. Some water molecules soak into the soil. They will sink deeper until they join the underground reservoir of ground water.

The molecule we have been following does not soak into the soil, but instead it flows along the ground until it reaches a creek. From there, it flows with trillions of other water molecules on a trip that ends in one of the oceans.

At any point along the way, the water molecule may begin the hydrologic cycle again. All it needs is enough energy to evaporate. (*Hydrologic cycle* is the name scientists give to the repeated path that water follows.)

Can you think of how the hydrologic cycle provides a continuous supply of fresh water for us to drink?

THE STORY—PART 4

An Alarming Situation

On March 26 and 27, 1994, weather forecasters issued numerous warnings about possible tornado conditions. As weather conditions worsened, those alerts were upgraded. Late-night advisories and early-morning warnings had heightened the public's awareness to the potential risks. Most of these timely warnings helped save lives. Unfortunately, the tornadoes came early in the morning and on a weekend, so there was a lack of storm spotters for the area. Storm spotters are trained volunteers who watch the skies for tornadoes and other severe weather.

The Weather Service Forecast Offices in Birmingham, Alabama, had issued a tornado warning for southern Cherokee County—the site of Goshen United Methodist Church. That alert was released 12 minutes before the fast-moving tornado struck the church. Five minutes later, a radio station in Cherokee County broadcast the Weather Service's tornado warning throughout the area. This radio alert was broadcast 7 minutes before the tornado impacted the church. But the tornado was traveling at up to 65 miles per hour. Few in its path heard the warnings.

Complicating the warning process in many of the tornado-struck areas was a lack of the National Oceanic and Atmospheric Administration's (NOAA) Weather Wire Service, the NWWS. This "voice of the National Weather Service" provides continuous and updated broadcasts of local weather. This service is transmitted via a network of special radio stations. These weather updates can be received on a simple and inexpensive radio receiver. Some of these radios have a standby mode that sounds an alarm in the event of severe weather. After the alarm sounds, the radio automatically switches on to receive voice updates. The Goshen church was not equipped with this kind of NOAA weather radio.

Furthermore, no emergency siren system existed near the church. Emergency sirens are set up in

STUDENT VOICES

After the tornado hit, we had no power for about two days. We got lanterns and flashlights to use. We couldn't play video games and we couldn't watch television. We could eat, though. I am in the Boy Scouts, and my dad and I go on camping trips. We knew what to do. We got out the grill and a skillet and cooked bacon for breakfast and fish for dinner.

At school, we have always had tornado drills. The tornado has made me take them more seriously. I don't play around as much any more. Now the people who survived the tornado want everybody to be quiet and just go where we are supposed to go.

JASON PRATER
PIEDMONT, ALABAMA

zones across the country. They send out a sound blast that can be heard around a 9.3-mile radius. A long, high-pitched siren indicates a tornado or weather alert. Either the weather radio system or the emergency siren system could have provided precious minutes to those in the church and elsewhere.

As a result of the Goshen tragedy, plans are now underway to expand and upgrade the emergency weather radio system for rural areas. The use of radios to receive weather warnings is expected to be as common as smoke detectors. In particular, places of public gathering are advised to be equipped with a tone-alert NOAA weather radio. Does your school have one? Should it?

Tornadoes are one of nature's most violent storms. To survive their fury, preparedness is the ultimate safety protection plan. Adequate shelters and warning systems are critical.

For those who lived through the Palm Sunday tornadoes, the loss of men, women, and children has been warning enough.

IN THE NEWS

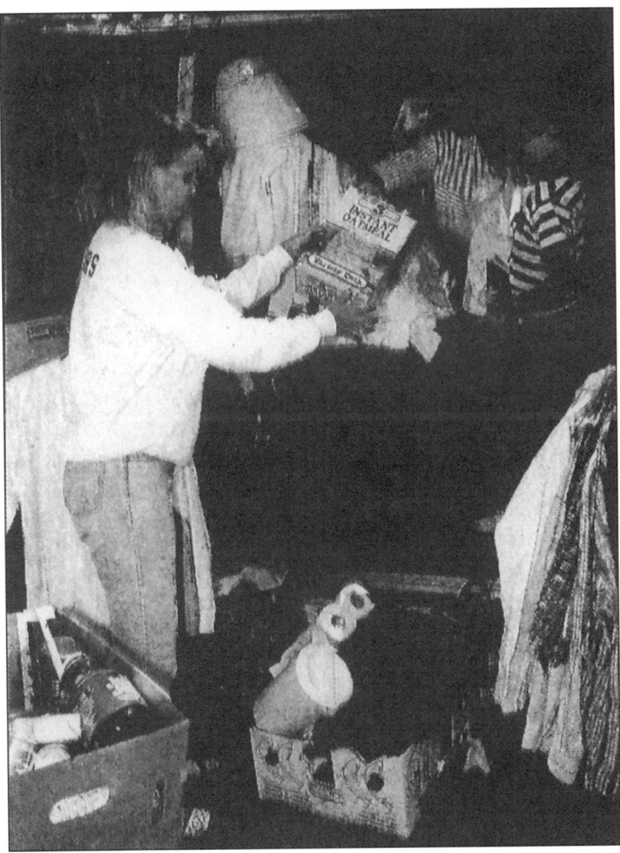

Steve Gross/The Anniston Star

Helping hands

Tamara Elders helps her daughter, Kathy Elders Plemons, left, and grandson Tyler Plemons unload relief goods that Mrs. Plemons brought up from Florida to aid tornado victims. Mrs. Plemons, a native of storm-ravaged Peeks Hill, gathered groceries and other items from her Orlando neighborhood and brought them north in her family's van. Story/12A.

Alabama will be first to receive expanded warning transmitters

By Richard Coe
Star Staff Writer

SPRING GARDEN — Alabama will be the first state to have its emergency weather radio signals expanded under a new federal program, a federal task force announced Monday.

After visiting tornado-damaged areas of northeast Alabama, Vice President Al Gore announced Thursday that the government will expand the National Weather Service's emergency radio transmissions. Twenty people died and more than 80 were injured when tornadoes struck the area last week.

Adam Golodner, acting deputy administrator of the Agriculture Department's Rural Electrification Administration, met with area officials at Spring Garden School Monday afternoon to discuss how to carry out the plan. He was joined by representatives from the Rural Development Administration, the Federal Emergency Management Agency and the National Weather Service.

"This is not something to wait for," Golodner said. "We'll make it happen this year."

Alabama has five of the emergency transmitters now, including one on Mount Cheaha that broadcast weather updates and give severe weather warnings.

Their signal can be picked up with a weather radio that can be purchased at most electronics stores for about $25. Some weather radios have a standby mode that buzzes during severe weather warnings and then automatically switches on.

But the problem in Alabama and other states is only a fraction of the population is close enough to a transmitter to pick up the signal. Nationwide, the coverage is estimated to be about 70 percent.

The plan is to upgrade Alabama's five transmitters to 1,000 watts and install three new transmitters, including one in the Fort Payne area. The new transmitters will have broadcast range of about 40 miles.

■ See Warnings/12A

ANNISTON STAR, APRIL 5, 1994

SCIENCE ACTIVITY

Wind Insurance

Purpose
To investigate the relationship between tornado frequency and intensity in the United States.

Background
You own a large national insurance company—HurtLess Insurance Corporation. Recent natural disasters have hit your customers hard. Your company has had to pay out a large number of claims. You have been losing a lot of money.

As tornado season approaches, you and the board of directors have decided to charge more for disaster insurance. First you need to determine which states are hardest hit by tornadoes. Then you will charge the customers in those states more for their disaster insurance.

The Discovery File "Tornado Data by State" on page 47 contains information to help you determine where to raise and where to lower disaster-insurance rates. Notice that it contains two kinds of information: average number of tornadoes annually per state and average number of tornadoes annually per 10,000 square miles (a square that is 100 miles by 100 miles). The 10,000-square-mile data takes into account the different sizes of the states to the nearest 10,000 square miles. Decide which set of data would be more useful in preparing a graph to rate each state's potential for tornado damage.

Materials

For each pair:
- Discovery File "Tornado Data by State" (from page 47)
- Map of the United States
- Cardboard
- Colored pencils
- Ruler
- Graph paper

Procedure
1. Prepare a visual display that shows the data you have chosen to plot.
2. Rate each state according to its potential for tornado damage. Use the following rating scale:
   ND = No risk of tornado damage. Extra insurance not needed. Damage covered under normal policy.
   WD = Low tornado risk. Wind-damage insurance needed.
   HD = High likelihood of costly tornado damage. High-cost tornado insurance is a necessity.
3. Compare your display with the display of someone who used the other set of data. Do they match? Why or why not? Which is better?

Conclusion
Each state has an insurance-rate commission. Your company must request permission from this commission to increase the rates you charge your customers. Decide with your group which set of data is more appropriate to use when you present your rate case to the commission. Write a description of the criteria you used to arrive at this decision.

IN THE NEWS

Improved forecasting in store for rural areas

The federal government today will unveil improvements in severe weather forecasting for rural areas, Vice President Gore told tornado victims Wednesday. The new system is expected to include satellite technology. Gore met with the Rev. Kelly Clem, pastor of Goshen United Methodist Church in Piedmont, Ala., where a tornado during Palm Sunday services killed 20, including Clem's daughter. Gore praised Clem and her husband for "the strength and grace you've shown through this." President Clinton declared Alabama a disaster area. The storm system that produced the tornadoes killed at least 43 people in Alabama, Georgia, Tennessee, North Carolina and South Carolina.

USA TODAY, THURSDAY, MARCH 31, 1994

DISCOVERY FILE

Tornado Data by State

State	Tornadoes per State	Tornadoes per 10,000 Sq. Mi.	State	Tornadoes per State	Tornadoes per 10,000 Sq. Mi.
Alabama	20	3.8	Montana	4	0.3
Alaska	0	0.0	Nebraska	35	4.6
Arizona	4	0.3	Nevada	1	0.1
Arkansas	20	3.7	New Hampshire	2	2.4
California	3	0.2	New Jersey	2	2.0
Colorado	19	1.5	New Mexico	8	0.7
Connecticut	2	3.0	New York	4	0.7
Delaware	1	4.5	North Carolina	12	2.2
Florida	41	6.6	North Dakota	17	2.3
Georgia	21	3.5	Ohio	14	3.4
Hawaii	1	0.9	Oklahoma	53	7.7
Idaho	1	0.2	Oregon	1	0.1
Illinois	27	4.9	Pennsylvania	8	1.6
Indiana	23	6.2	Rhode Island	0	0.3
Iowa	27	4.6	South Carolina	9	3.0
Kansas	43	5.5	South Dakota	24	3.0
Kentucky	8	2.0	Tennessee	11	2.7
Louisiana	20	4.1	Texas	119	4.4
Maine	3	0.8	Utah	1	0.2
Maryland	3	2.4	Vermont	1	1.0
Massachusetts	4	4.9	Virginia	6	1.4
Michigan	16	2.7	Washington	1	0.2
Minnesota	18	0.2	West Virginia	2	0.8
Mississippi	22	4.7	Wisconsin	18	3.0
Missouri	27	4.1	Wyoming	9	0.8

Source: NOAA

IN THE NEWS

In Alabama, a 'healing' service

Congregation prays amid church ruins

By Sandra Sanchez
USA TODAY

Harold Price couldn't sing in the choir loft on Easter as he has for so many years at Goshen United Methodist Church.

Instead, Price, 80, lifted his voice to the heavens from a metal folding chair in the parking lot of the Piedmont, Ala., church that was destroyed Palm Sunday by a tornado.

Seated beside him during the windy and chilly sunrise service were 200 other parishioners who had survived the tornado that killed 20 worshipers, including six children.

"It was worthwhile, very healing," said Price, who attended services with his daughter Faye Studdard, 44, who had pulled him from beneath the rubble last Sunday. "The emotions were so high."

Cars lined roads for blocks around the church, parts of which stood in the background as an eerie reminder.

During the service, parishioners hugged, held hands, cried and reaffirmed their faith in God and the close-knit community of 5,000 residents.

Some were on crutches. Many had bandaged limbs.

Marcus Woods, 13 — whose father, Buddy, and sister, Amy, 9, had been killed — was in a wheelchair. "I just wanted to be here," Woods said shivering in the chilly air.

"There's no place I'd rather be today," a badly bruised Rev. Kelly Clem told those gathered. "Nor life, nor angels, nor rulers, nor things present, nor things to come . . . nor anything else in all creation will ever be able to separate us."

Clem, whose daughter Hannah, 4, was killed in the twister, led a special sermon for the surviving children and gave each an Easter basket. The baskets — along with money, food and clothing — were donated by churches and well-wishers from across the USA.

A wooden cross behind Clem's pulpit was made by a friend she hadn't seen in years, she said. And four new stained glass windows were donated by a Catholic church.

"I feel like we're like a symbol of hope," Clem said.

By Dave Martin, AP

IN PIEDMONT, ALA.: Faye Studdard, in glasses, hugs Debra Hamrick after a sunrise service outside Goshen United Methodist Church. A week ago, 20 people died when a tornado hit the church.

"We feel like we all need each other right now. And that's why I look forward to every Sunday," said Donna Tyree, 18. Tyree's great-aunt, Adell Kiser, 96, was still hospitalized since having her left leg amputated following the storm. "We just feel like we all need to be together."

Missing from the Easter service was Price's wife, Reba, 66, who suffered an injured breastbone when the church's roof collapsed onto her pew.

But Reba's absence didn't prevent Price from singing louder than ever Sunday.

"There's going to be some deep scars," he said. "We're going to rebuild and we're going to be stronger and better."

Brandenburg, Ky., Mayor Carl Wells empathized.

Wells' town of 1,857 residents Sunday commemorated the 20th anniversary of a tornado that killed 31 people, leveled homes, businesses, a church. The tornado also killed 32 people in Xenia, Ohio.

Sunday, Wells and about 75 others attended a ceremony at the Meade County Courthouse, where the names of Brandenburg's dead were read.

"I have all the sympathy for that bunch in (Piedmont), Ala., because I know what they're going through," said Wells. "It's just a tremendous task to come back, but we've made it."

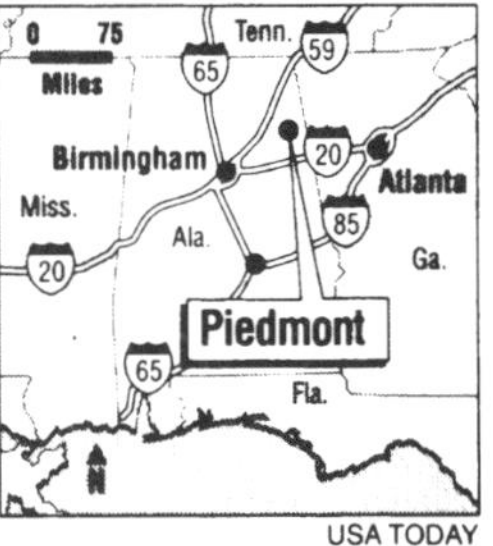

USA TODAY

Holiday events around USA and the world

Easter elsewhere:

▶ In Santa Monica, Calif., about 1,500 worshipers held services in a tent in the parking lot of St. Monica's Catholic Church. A magnitude 6.8 earthquake Jan. 17 caused $5 million damage to the 67-year-old church. "We sit in this beautiful tent and say: Hallelujah! It's Easter!" the Rev. Douglas Glassman said.

▶ In Washington, an AIDS activist demanding more research funding disrupted Easter services for President Clinton and his family at the Foundry United Methodist Church. "Save your prayers for Bill Clinton. . . . Bill Clinton lied!" shouted a man who calls himself Luke Sissyfag. He also disrupted a Clinton speech in December.

▶ In New York, Easter garb was displayed in a 25-block-long pedestrian parade on Fifth Avenue marked by odd and oversized hats. "People keep asking me, 'Where are the floats?' " said police officer Daniel Valenza.

▶ Pope John Paul II told the 60,000 people in St. Peter's Square at the Vatican that he hoped the joy of Christianity's most important holiday would overwhelm violence and hate.

▶ In Seoul, South Korea, a man reportedly angered at being refused an interview with Cardinal Kim Sou Hwan grabbed the prelate and pushed him down. Church officials overpowered the assailant; the cardinal, 71, wasn't injured.

— From wire reports

USA TODAY, APRIL 4, 1994

DISCOVERY FILE

Waterspouts, Landspouts, and Dust Devils

A waterspout is a weak tornado that generally forms between the bottom of a cloud and the surface of a body of warm water. Waterspouts are most common along the coast of the Gulf of Mexico and southeastern United States. In the western states, they can occur with cold, late fall or late winter storms. These are times when tornado development is least expected.

Waterspouts can also begin as violent whirling eddies whipping up from the water's surface. When waterspouts sometimes venture onto land, they become tornadoes. The term *landspout* is used to describe another type of tornado that tends to be relatively weak.

Dust devils generally form in the desert from columns of hot air whirling up from the ground. They do not have the strength of tornadoes, but they still can cause damage. Whirling winds can also occur over snow. Would you call them snow devils or snow angels?

IN THE NEWS

Amerson: 911 can give fair warning

By Laura Tutor
Star Staff Writer

The head of Calhoun County's 911 service said he and other 911 administrators want to meet with the National Weather Service to clear up any confusion about what their agencies need to do during a tornado.

Larry Amerson took issue with a complaint a weather service meteorologist made at a meeting in Birmingham Monday. The meteorologist said if his agency had been notified that an actual tornado had developed from the storm cell it had been tracking, warnings about the twister could have been made sooner. More than 100 calls were made to 911 and other emergency offices about the tornado, the meteorologist said, but no reports reached the weather service.

As it was, the deadly tornado that swept across northeast Alabama had been on the ground almost an hour — and had killed 22 people — before the weather service knew about it.

Amerson, whose Anniston office received 87 emergency calls about storm damage on March 27, said he didn't know the weather service expected 911 or any other emergency agency to call and report a tornado sighting. "If they wanted 911 systems to notify them," Amerson said Wednesday, "they should tell us."

He sent a letter later that day to meteorologist Brian Peters inviting the weather service to a statewide 911 meeting to coordinate a communication policy for tornados or other weather disasters.

In fact, Amerson said in a press release, the weather service was probably one of the few agencies 911 didn't call about the storm. Soon after the tornado plowed through the northern part of the county around 11:30 a.m., 911 operators talked with law enforcement and emergency workers in areas including Ohatchee,

■ See Warning/11A

County to get 10 new sirens

All of Calhoun County will be included in the emergency warning system after 10 new sirens are added to those already in place, said Delois Champ, spokesperson for the Calhoun County Emergency Management Agency.

The additional sirens, which will go in the northern part of the county and the DeArmanville/White Plains area in the eastern section of the county, were requested in response to the deadly Palm Sunday tornado that tore through the Piedmont area.

The Federal Emergency Management Agency in Washington approved including the rest of the county in the warning system Tuesday. Mrs. Champ didn't know this morning when the sirens will be in place.

"I don't have a definite date on it," she said. "Hopefully in the near future."

Seven sirens will go in the northern county areas, and three more will cover the eastern part. If tests show that more sirens are needed, they will be requested, Mrs. Champ said.

— **Laura Tutor**

ANNISTON STAR, APRIL 14, 1994

ON THE JOB

Warnings-Coordination Meteorologist

Reneé Fair
National Weather Service
Little Rock, Arkansas

As a child growing up in South Carolina, I always liked to walk in the rain. I liked to watch thunderstorms, too. When I was in the eleventh grade, my chemistry teacher really turned me on to science. Now I am a warnings-coordination meteorologist (WCM) for the National Weather Service Forecast Office in Little Rock, Arkansas.

If you are interested in weather forecasting, work hard in all of your classes now. You can become a forecaster by studying meteorology or by first getting a degree in math or physics. Meteorology courses I took in college had such titles as "Dynamic Meteorology," "Climatology," and "Physical Meteorology."

Did you know that weather forecasters are allowed to do something that ordinary people cannot do? Every meteorologist who works in a National Weather Service Office can fly in the cockpit of any commercial airliner. It is part of a familiarization flight program.

A WCM's main job is marketing, public relations, and outreach programs. As the warnings-coordination meteorologist, I develop education programs for the community, and I help people deal with laws that relate to severe weather. I also meet with each county's emer-

gency manager to find out that county's unique problems. That helps us do a better job of helping them during severe storm or tornado watches and warnings.

I also evaluate emergency preparedness. I make sure the state is ready to respond quickly when severe weather or tornadoes strike.

When I come to the office each day, my main focus is what the emergency managers need that day. Usually they want to schedule spotters' training sessions. We have between 6,000 and 9,000 spotters in Arkansas. Many of them are amateur (HAM) radio operators. Spotters are also state police, highway patrol officers, emergency medical technicians, ambulance drivers, firefighters, road crews, and interested citizens. Anyone whose job is outside can be a spotter. Junior-high students can also become spotters. All you need to do is take spotter training from the National Weather Service Office near you.

Safety officers at factories and manufacturing companies often ask me to come in and speak to their employees. We provide weather preparedness and safety programs and sometimes spotter training. A company that has 100 people working in a warehouse needs to have a safety plan. The employees must know the safest place in the building during a tornado or severe storm. Employees also need training in evacuation and other emergency procedures. Coordinating all these programs keeps me busy.

My advice to you in doing your task is to make sure you are working with reliable information. Ideally, you want to have as much "ground truth" as you can get. Compare the ground observations with the Doppler radar.

As you and your team are monitoring the weather data, you will receive information showing that something has actually occurred. You need to ask these questions: Where was it sighted? How fast was it moving? Which areas are going to be affected?

Your forecast office will be a very busy place when severe storm warnings are in effect. People want immediate updates. Weather reports are being written. The NOAA Weather Radio announcer is broadcasting. Don't forget, when your report goes out on the news, you have to make sure that it will be easily understood by the public. Saving lives depends on you and your team.

I still have a lot of respect for the weather, but I do not worry about it raining on my picnic any more.

Weather conditions have been changing over the decades. Why is one area getting more rain than another area? Why is the jet stream further south this season than it was last season? Some meteorologists are involved in research and development. They report that changes and trends in our climate can be influenced by such factors as El Niño, sunspots, and depletion of the ozone layer.

IN THE NEWS

A community rebuilds

Tornado a blow to Goshen pride

By Jenny Cromie
Star Staff Writer

GOSHEN — The tornado ripped the roof off Johnny Gossett's house and stole most of his worldly possessions. But what hurt worst was the loss of his pride.

"Forty-five years old and I never asked for anything," Gossett said in front of his mangled home Wednesday. "If I didn't have it, I've done without."

That stubborn independence kept Gossett away from the relief center set up for tornado victims this week. He sought help instead from relatives nearby. It wasn't until his daughter, Michelle Gossett, contacted volunteers that the family got the help it needed.

Wednesday, Gossett's son, Jeffrey, joined hundreds of tornado survivors who trooped through the Piedmont Civic Center gymnasium, picking up clothes, food and other donated items to help them through the aftermath of the storm.

Meanwhile, outside the gym, LaVonne McGee of the East Alabama Planning Commission was getting ready to deliver blankets, toilet paper, laundry detergent and an assortment of other donated items to Gossett. Volunteers also were trying to find him a trailer to live in.

"He's never had to ask for anything before," Ms. McGee said of Gossett. "It has broken his pride, I guess you could say."

Gossett is not alone. The storms Sunday left hundreds of normally self-sufficient people in need of help.

In addition to the toll on human life — 22 killed and 157 injured — most of them when the tornado flattened Goshen United Methodist Church during a Palm Sunday service — the storms destroyed 108 houses and 275 mobile homes and damaged 1,052 houses and 17 mobile homes. Eighty-six businesses

■ See Rebuild 6A

Vice president Al Gore, flanked by the Rev. Kelly Clem and the Rev. Dale Clem, right, and Gov. Jim Folsom, Jr., talks of warnings proposal Wednesday at Goshen disaster site.

Ken Elkins/The Anniston Star

Rural areas will get weather warnings

By Sarah Pekkanen
States News Service

WASHINGTON — Vice President Al Gore today announced a plan to expand emergency weather radio signals into rural areas in hopes of avoiding future tragedies such as the killer tornado that struck northeast Alabama.

The goal is to extend the National Weather Service's radio warning system to 95 percent of Americans. The weather service's 350-station network now reaches about 75 percent of the population.

"In high risk areas, (the radios) will soon be as common as smoke detectors," Gore said.

Priority will be given to "tornado alley and coastal areas at risk from hurricanes," Gore said. The system will include warnings of all types of disasters, not just threatening weather, he said.

Gore's announcement comes one day after he visited the wreckage of the Goshen United Methodist Church, where 20 parishioners were killed and dozens injured when a tornado struck during services Sunday. Although forecasters gave about 17 minutes' warning before the tornado struck, the weather radio system does not reach the Goshen area and church members were not aware of the impending storm.

During his visit to the area Wednesday, Gore said "one of the lessons our nation must learn from this tragedy is we must do a better job of providing severe weather warnings to comm unities."

On his visit, Gore met the Rev. Kelly Clem, pastor of the Goshen church, and her minister husband, whose daughter was killed in the tornado. On the "Today" show this morning, Gore said "I'm in awe of the strength of Rev. Kelly Clem and Rev. Dale Clem."

He described the Clems as "really incredible folks."

In announcing plans for the improved warning ststem, Gore said, "The weak link in the chain was the inability to get the warning information to all of the people in the threatened area."

■ See Warning 7A

ANNISTON STAR, TUESDAY, MARCH 29, 1994

Technology Education: Cheap Success

Purpose

To construct devices that measure wind speed and direction.

Background

Congratulations! You have graduated from college! But the job market is tight, especially in the field of meteorology.

Radio station WCHP (the disk jockeys call it W-CHEAP) in Topeka, Kansas, has hired you as weather forecaster. There's just one problem: you want to put out top-quality weather forecasts, but the station's budget will not allow it. Doppler radar? Forget it! They don't even have a computer for you to use or a satellite downlink to help you predict the weather.

When you asked the station manager about getting some equipment, she said, "Call the National Weather Service and read their forecast. That's what the last guy did." When you replied that you wanted your own instruments, she gave you $100.

Of course you were not happy with this outcome, but you started thinking about some of the things you learned in school. Wind speed and direction seemed to be a good place to start. With a budget of $100, you went to the local hardware store to buy the items you needed to build an anemometer and a weather vane. With these two instruments, at least you will have some information about conditions in Topeka. Who knows, if this works, you may even get money to build a rain gauge!

Your assignment is to research the anemometer and weather vane to understand their purposes and how they operate. Then you will design and build an anemometer and weather vane using some or all of the materials listed.

Materials

For the anemometer:

- 3 small paper, plastic, or plastic foam cups
- 1 bicycle-pedal bearing unit
- A motor and/or generator
- Insulated electric wire
- Wooden dowel rods or metal rods
- 1 voltmeter or a meter calibrated to miles per hour
- A base or stand of whatever material is suitable
- Graph paper

For the weather vane:

- Plywood or pressed board, ¼ inch thick, for the indicator arrow
- 1 PVC pipe, 2 inches in diameter
- 1 PVC pipe, 1¾ inches in diameter
- Small pieces of brass or other material to be an electrical connector
- Low-voltage insulated electrical wire
- 4 low-voltage lightbulbs and sockets
- Wooden dowel rods or metal rods
- 1 9-volt battery
- Small brass screws and nuts (Note: Any conducting materials may be used.)
- 1 on/off switch
- A base or stand
- A box or container for the lightbulbs
- A label maker or markers
- Graph paper

Note: The above materials are for building a weather vane with a remote light board to indicate wind direction. Your teacher might ask you to build a basic weather vane without lights instead. If this happens, the materials list will be altered by your teacher. Also, if you are using electricity, allow enough wire so the weather vane can be outdoors and the light board can be indoors. If you are going to use any materials not in your laboratory, get your teacher's permission before you begin.

Procedure

1. Investigate construction procedures for both instruments. Determine the process you and/or your group will use to complete this activity.
2. Gather appropriate materials.
3. Use graph paper to make necessary patterns.
4. Use all tools and machines safely and in a manner approved by your teacher.
5. After constructing the parts, file, drill, and sand them.
6. Before assembling, make certain all necessary parts are completed.
7. Make certain you know what procedures will be followed before you start assembling.
8. After completing the devices, calibrate any meters used.

9. Test your devices. Make modifications as needed.

Conclusions

1. Now that your instruments are up and running at WCHP, what information have you been able to gather? What conclusions have been made for the people of Topeka?
2. What is an anemometer? What task does it perform? Were you able to calibrate it accurately? If so, how?
3. What is *windchill factor*?
4. How accurate is your weather vane? What did you learn from it?
5. If you used electrical components on your weather vane, what did you learn about electricity and magnetism? Are they related? If so, how? Are the lamps connected in a series circuit or parallel circuit? What is the advantage and disadvantage of each method?
6. What problems, if any, did you encounter during the construction phase of this activity?
7. What problems, if any, did you have when using the instruments you built?
8. If you had the opportunity to do this activity again, what would you do differently?

INTERDISCIPLINARY ACTIVITY

Social Studies: The State of Risk

Purpose

To prepare a color-coded map of the United States showing tornado occurrences; to develop a ranking of states according to their risk of tornado occurrences.

Background

Tornadoes are responsible for more deaths annually than any other natural phenomenon except lightning. Tornado surface winds can exceed 300 miles per hour. They are the strongest winds on the earth. You and your team of meteorologists are interested in gathering data on tornado formation. Deciding where to place the base of your operation is the first step. By selecting a location where tornado formation is common, your team will be able to gather first-hand information. Quick response is crucial. Tornadoes do not last very long.

Materials

For each student:

- Isogram map (from teacher)
- Atlas or textbook with maps of the United States
- Colored pencils

Procedure

You and your team will receive information about tornadoes in the United States. The information is in the form of a map with isograms.

1. Color-code the map, and then compare it with a political map of the United States. Select a state where you wish to build the base for your tornado-response team.
2. Place a star in that state, and be prepared to give a logical reason for your choice.
3. Using the same data and map, determine the degree of tornado risk for each state. Classify states as either high risk, moderate risk, or little to no risk. Sometimes, deciding a state's risk of tornadoes will be easy. But sometimes it will take careful observation and consideration, because the isograms do not follow state boundaries. Your team's risk assessment is very important. It will determine what safety measures each state will have to take.

INTERDISCIPLINARY ACTIVITY

Math: Tornadoes and Line Graphs

Purpose

To interpret data about tornadoes from multiple-line graphs.

Background

Very high winds and flying debris make every tornado a potential killer. But although they often leave paths of death and destruction, sometimes tornadoes are harmless. Factors that help determine the amount of damage and number of deaths include the time of year tornadoes occur, their location, and the population density where they occur.

Materials

- "Tornado Incidence by Month" graph

Procedure

You are the statistician (statistics expert) on a team that is studying the relationship between time of year and the number of tornado deaths. You have already collected data from the past 30 years and displayed them on a multiple-line graph. All that's left is the analysis of the data and your report to the commission investigating tornado deaths.

Analyze the multiple-line graph (above, right). Search for tendencies and trends that are likely to influence commission decisions. But remember, you must be able to justify your conclusions.

Tornado Incidence by Month

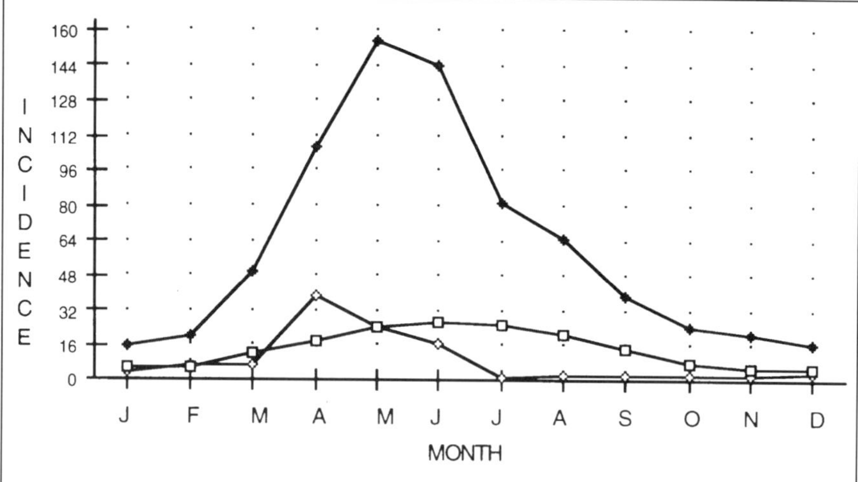

Conclusion

Prepare a five-minute presentation of your findings for the Tornado Fatality Commission (TFC). Try to summarize your findings in one paragraph, and use graphics to illustrate the points you make. One team will be selected at random to make the actual presentation. Unless a team disputes the conclusions presented, all other teams will simply turn in their paragraphs and graphics. When the presentation is finished, you may want to discuss other factors that could have influenced the timing of the deaths.

Interdisciplinary Activity

English: Tornado in a Letter

Purpose

To write a friendly letter describing a tornado.

Background

Imagine you are a teenager who was living in Goshen, Alabama, on the day the tornado struck. A friend of yours in another part of the country has never seen a tornado. You decide to write a letter telling your friend what it was like being in a tornado.

Before you begin writing, there are a number of topics you should consider. Who were you with and what were you doing when the tornado struck? What happened before you saw the tornado? What did you see as the tornado approached? What happened as the tornado hit, and what happened immediately after?

In addition to narrating the events, you should pay attention to what you were thinking and feeling at each stage of the tornado. Make sure your final product follows the format of a friendly letter.

Procedure

As you write, you may want to begin by using a graphic organizer to generate and organize details. Such an organizer might be a web, an outline, a chart, or a list.

Use the information in your organizer to write the first draft. Read your first draft silently to evaluate it. Use the revision questions below to guide your self-evaluation. Ask some of your peers to read your draft, using the same questions to offer you further suggestions.

Write a second draft using both your own suggestions and those of your peers. Look over your work a final time. Look for errors in spelling, punctuation, and mechanics.

Use the questions below to help you revise your first draft.

1. Did you write a letter that follows the friendly letter format?
2. What details show how the event began? What other details can you add?
3. What details tell what happened during the tornado? What other details might you include?
4. What details describe the aftermath of the tornado? What other details might you add?
5. Did you mention your feelings and reactions at each stage of your letter?

PERFORMANCE ASSESSMENT

Tornado Commercials

Purpose

To write a radio script about the risk from tornadoes.

Background

Because so many of the victims of the tornado in Goshen, Alabama, were children and teenagers, the governor has decided the state must take steps to better educate young people about the dangers of tornadoes. As the youth liaison of the state's Department of Public Safety, you have been asked by the governor to develop a script for a 30-second radio commercial aimed at young people between 12 and 18 years old.

This commercial, which will play on popular radio stations, should inform young people about tornadoes. Before you write, think about the three different areas the governor has asked you to address:

- What are the warning signs of tornadoes?
- What should you do in a tornado?
- What should you do immediately after a tornado?

Procedure

Once you have thought about the information that should be included in the commercial, organize it so it is logically and clearly presented. Think about how you will get the attention of your audience. Finally, your script should show that you are knowledgeable about tornadoes and are able to communicate that knowledge to young people.

Begin by using a graphic organizer to generate and organize details. Such an organizer might be a web, an outline, a chart, or a list. Use the information in your organizer to write a first draft.

Read your first draft silently as you evaluate it. Have you included all important information? What details are missing, or what information can you add? Ask some classmates to evaluate your rough draft using the Peer-Response Form from page 57.

Write a second draft using both your suggestions and those of your peers. Look over your work one last time for errors in spelling, punctuation, and mechanics.

As you think about and write your script, you should keep these points in mind:

1. Catch your readers' attention.
2. Address each of the three areas suggested by the governor.
3. Keep your audience in mind.
4. Select the most important information, and use it to create an effective presentation.
5. Write a script that is easy to understand and follow.

Use the questions below to help you revise your first draft.

1. Is your script aimed at teenagers?
2. How does your script get the listeners' attention?
3. What tornado warning signs are included in your script? What other warning signs should you add?
4. What does your script tell listeners to do during a tornado? What other steps might be taken?
5. According to your script, what should your listeners do immediately after a tornado?
6. What parts of your script could you rearrange to organize it more clearly?

Peer-Response Form

Directions

1. Ask your partners to listen carefully as you read your rough draft aloud.
2. Ask your partners to help you improve your writing by telling you the answers to the questions below.
3. Jot down notes about what your partners say.

   a. What did you like best about my rough draft?

   b. What did you have the hardest time understanding about my rough draft?

   c. What can you suggest that I do to improve my rough draft?

4. Exchange rough drafts with a partner. In pencil, place a check mark near any mechanical, spelling, or grammatical constructions about which you are uncertain. Return the papers and check your own. Ask your partner for clarification if you do not understand or agree with the comments on your paper. Jot down notes you will want to remember when writing your revision.

Proofreading Guidesheet

1. Have you identified the assigned purpose of the writing assignment and have you accomplished that purpose?

2. Have you written on the assigned topic?

3. Have you identified the assigned form your writing should take and written accordingly?

4. Have you addressed the assigned audience in your writing?

5. Have you used sentences of different lengths and types to make your writing effective?

6. Have you chosen language carefully so the reader understands what you mean?

7. Have you done the following to make your writing clear for someone else to read:
   - used appropriate capitalization?
   - kept pronouns clear?
   - kept verb tense consistent?
   - made sure all words are spelled correctly?
   - used correct punctuation?
   - used complete sentences?
   - made all subjects and verbs agree?
   - organized your ideas into logical paragraphs?

APPENDIX

Weather Observations for 4:00 P.M. (Central Daylight Time)

ALO Waterloo, IA. Overcast, visibility 3 miles in rain. Pressure 1000.5 mb, temperature 62, dew point 61, wind from 310 at 20 mph.

AMA Amarillo, TX. Overcast, visibility 2 miles in rain shower. Pressure 1013.5 mb, temperature 80, dew point 62, wind from 200 at 30 mph.

BUB Broken Bow, NB. Clear, visibility 30 miles. Pressure 1014.0 mb, temperature 44, dew point 32, wind from 330 at 10 mph.

CNK Concordia, KS. Broken clouds, visibility 6 miles. Pressure 1008.5 mb, temperature 62, dew point 47, wind from 310 at 15 mph.

CNU Chanute Air Force Base, KS. Partly cloudy, visibility 10 miles. Pressure 1009.0 mb, temperature 88, dew point 70, wind from 225 at 20 mph.

DDC Dodge City, KS. Partly cloudy, visibility 40 miles. Pressure 1011.0 mb, temperature 69, dew point 49, wind from 310 at 20 mph.

DSM Des Moines, IA. Overcast, visibility 5 miles in rain. Pressure 1001.5 mb, temperature 66, dew point 64, wind from 280 at 20 mph.

FSM Ft. Smith, AR. Scattered clouds, visibility 5 miles in haze. Pressure 1016.5 mb, temperature 97, dew point 74, wind from 230 at 5 mph.

GAG Gage, OK. Broken clouds, visibility 10 miles. Pressure 1012.0 mb, temperature 81, dew point 50, wind from 220 at 15 mph.

GCK Garden City, KS. Scattered clouds, visibility 40 miles. Pressure 1013.0 mb, temperature 61, dew point 45, wind from 315 at 25 mph.

GLD Goodland, KS. Clear, visibility 40 miles. Pressure 1015.5 mb, temperature 50, dew point 34, wind from 340 at 15 mph.

GRI Grand Island, NB. Scattered clouds, visibility 20 miles. Pressure 1012.0 mb, temperature 50, dew point 36, wind from 320 at 10 mph.

HLC Hill City, KS. Scattered clouds, visibility 30 miles. Pressure 1012.5 mb, temperature 55, dew point 42, wind from 320 at 20 mph.

ICT Wichita, KS. Sky obscured, visibility ½ mile in thunderstorm. Pressure 1008.0 mb, temperature 80, dew point 71, wind from 200 at 30 mph. **Remarks:** Tornado sighted 2 miles west of airport, moving northeast at 45 mph.

LBF North Platte, NB. Clear, visibility 25 miles. Pressure 1016.5 mb, temperature 45, dew point 33, wind from 315 at 10 mph.

30I Lamoni, IA. Overcast, visibility 3 miles in rain shower. Pressure 1002.0 mb, temperature 70, dew point 65, wind from 260 at 25 mph.

LTS Altus, OK. Partly cloudy, visibility 25 miles. Pressure 1014.5 mb, temperature 89, dew point 54, wind from 240 at 20 mph. **Remarks:** Thunderstorm ended in past hour.

MCI Kansas City, MO. Broken clouds, visibility 15 miles. Pressure 1004.5 mb, temperature 82, dew point 71, wind from 225 at 15 mph. **Remarks:** Thunderstorm approaching station.

MLC McAlester, OK. Clear, visibility 6 miles in haze. Pressure 1018.0 mb, temperature 98, dew point 73, wind from 210 at 10 mph.

OFK Norfolk, NB. Scattered clouds, visibility 25 miles. Pressure 1011.0 mb, temperature 48, dew point 36, wind from 330 at 10 mph.

OKC Oklahoma City, OK. Partly cloudy, visibility 10 miles. Pressure 1015.0 mb, temperature 92, dew point 71, wind from 225 at 20 mph.

OMA Omaha, NB. Partly cloudy, visibility 10 miles. Pressure 1007.0 mb, temperature 59, dew point 45, wind from 300 at 20 mph.

PNC Ponca City, OK. Partly cloudy, visibility 10 miles. Pressure 1012.0 mb, temperature 89, dew point 72, wind from 210 at 15 mph. **Remarks:** Thunderstorm approaching station.

SLN Salina, KS. Overcast, visibility 10 miles. Pressure 1007.5 mb, temperature 69, dew point 57, wind from 300 at 20 mph. **Remarks:** Thunderstorm ended in past hour.

STJ St. Joseph, MO. Overcast, visibility 4 miles in thunderstorm. Pressure 1003.5 mb, temperature 68, dew point 66, wind from 260 at 15 mph.

SUX Sioux City, IA. Scattered clouds, visibility 15 miles. Pressure 1008.0 mb, temperature 50, dew point 38, wind from 320 at 15 mph.

TOP Topeka, KS. Sky obscured, visibility 0 miles in thunderstorm with hail. Pressure 1005.0 mb, temperature 75, dew point 72, wind from 225 at 45 mph.

TUL Tulsa, OK. Scattered clouds, visibility 15 miles in haze. Pressure 1014.0 mb, temperature 93, dew point 72, wind from 225 at 10 mph.

VTN Valentine, NB. Clear, visibility 20 miles. Pressure 1016.5 mb, temperature 43, dew point 31, wind from 350 at 5 mph.

RESOURCES

Books on Tornadoes

Armbruster, Ann, and Elizabeth A. Taylor. *Tornadoes.* New York: Franklin Watts, 1993.

Kramer, Stephen. *Lightning.* Minneapolis: The Lerner Group, 1993.

———. *Tornado.* Minneapolis: The Lerner Group, 1992.

Lampton, Christopher. *Tornado.* Brookfield, Conn.: Millbrook Press, 1991.

Lockhart, Gary. *The Weather Companion: An Album of Meteorological History, Science, Legend, and Folklore.* New York: John Wiley & Sons, Inc., 1988.

Williams, Jack. *USA TODAY Weather Book.* New York: Random House, 1992.

Also refer to books on lightning by Martin Uman of the University of Florida.

Other books on weather:

Cosgrove, Brian. *Weather.* New York: Alfred A. Knopf Books for Young Readers, 1991.

Goodman, Billy. *Natural Wonders and Disasters.* New York: Little, Brown & Co., 1991.

Lambert, David, and Ralph Hardy. *Weather and Its Work.* New York: Facts on File Publications, 1987.

Lane, Frank W. *The Violent Earth.* Topsfield, Mass.: Salem House, 1986.

Purvis, George, and Anne Purvis. *Weather and Climate.* New York: Bookwright Press, 1984.

Simon, Seymour. *Storms.* New York: Morrow Junior Books, 1989.

Information about tornadoes and weather is also available from

The Tornado Project; Thomas Grazulis, Director; P.O. Box 302, St. Johnsbury, Vermont 05819; (802) 748-2505; excellent videos, posters, and other resources on tornadoes.

National Weather Service Public Affairs Office; 11325 East-West Highway, Silver Spring, Maryland 20910.

American Meteorological Society; 1701 K Street N.W., Suite 300, Washington, D.C. 20006.

National Center for Atmospheric Research, Information and Education Outreach Program; P.O. Box 3000, Boulder, Colorado 80307-3000; (303) 497-8600.

National Climatic Data Center; Federal Building, Asheville, North Carolina 28801.

Tornado Tube (Make your own tornado with two clear plastic soda bottles and this attachment). $2.95 to Tornado Tube; 26 Dearborn St., Salem, Massachusetts 01970; (508) 745-1788.

Weatherwise, a bimonthly magazine for nonscientists who are interested in weather. Heldref Publications; 1319 18th Street N.W., Washington, D.C. 20036.

Acknowledgments

Author
Russell G. Wright, with contributions from Barbara Sprungman, Leonard David, and the following teachers:

Science Activities
*William Krayer, Gaithersburg High School, Gaithersburg, Maryland
*Frank S. Weisel, Tilden Middle School, Rockville, Maryland.

Interdisciplinary Activities
*Bernard Hudock, Watkins Mill High School, Gaithersburg, Maryland
*Jeanne S. Klugel, John F. Kennedy High School, Silver Spring, Maryland
*John Senuta, Ridgeview Middle School, Gaithersburg, Maryland
*Joseph Panarella, Montgomery Village Middle School, Gaithersburg, Maryland
*Nancy Carey, Col. E. Brooke Lee Middle School, Silver Spring, Maryland
*Charles Doebler, Robert Frost Middle School, Rockville, Maryland
*Nell Jeter, Earle B. Wood Middle School, Rockville, Maryland
*Richard Knight, Baker Middle School, Damascus, Maryland
*Gene Molesky, Ridgeview Middle School, Gaithersburg, Maryland
*Sheila Shillinger, Montgomery Village Middle School, Gaithersburg, Maryland
*Thomas Smith, Briggs Chaney Middle School, Silver Spring, Maryland
*Robert McDowell, Albert Einstein High School, Kensington, Maryland

Teacher/Writer Interns
Kelly Hortch, University of Maryland, College Park, Maryland
Donna Obermeier, University of Maryland, College Park, Maryland

Geology Advisor
Evan Wolff, Northern Arizona University, Flagstaff, Arizona

Event/Site Support
Sherry Kughn, Oxford, Alabama
Kim Davis, head librarian, Piedmont Public Library, Piedmont, Alabama
Megan Johnson, Piedmont Public Library, Piedmont, Alabama

Scientific Reviews
William O. Alexander, National Oceanic and Atmospheric Administration
Dorothy K. Hall, National Aeronautics and Space Administration
Frederick P. Ostby, National Oceanic and Atmospheric Administration

Student Consultants
*Redland Middle School, Rockville, Maryland: Antonio Balingit, Jr., Haroun Hebron, David Huang, Mary Hunter, Anna Krebs, Paul Little, Jacquelyn Martin, Jessica Minera, Angela Moore, Joi Pearson, Sarah Pettit, Geoff Reed, Meredith Saladyga, Stevie Sickles
*John T. Baker Middle School, Damascus, Maryland: Joel Krayer

Field-Test Teachers
Judith Basile, Agawam Junior High School, Feeding Hills, Massachusetts
Mark Carlson, Westlane Middle School, Indianapolis, Indiana
Adrianne Criminger, Lanier Middle School, Buford, Georgia
Cheryl Glotfelty, Northern Middle School, Accident, Maryland
Linda Mosser, Northern Middle School, Accident, Maryland
David Needham, Albert Einstein Middle School, Sacramento, California
Annette Newsome, West Baltimore Middle School, Baltimore, Maryland
Amy Resler, Westlane Middle School, Indianapolis, Indiana
Karen Shugrue, Agawam Junior High School, Feeding Hills, Massachusetts
Gloria Yost, Albert Einstein Middle School, Sacramento, California

EBS Advisory Committee
Dr. Eddie Anderson, National Aeronautic and Space Administration
Ms. Mary Ann Brearton, American Association for the Advancement of Science
Dr. Lynn Dierking, Science Learning, Inc.
Mr. Bob Dubill, *USA Today*
Mr. Herbert Freiberger, United States Geological Survey
Ms. Joyce Gross, National Oceanic and Atmospheric Administration
Dr. Harry Herzer, National Aeronautic and Space Administration
Dr. Frank Ireton, American Geophysical Union
*Mr. Bill Krayer, Gaithersburg High School, Gaithersburg, Maryland
Dr. Rocky Lopes, American Red Cross
*Dr. Jerry Lynch, John T. Baker Middle School, Damascus, Maryland
Ms. Virginia Major, United States Geological Survey
Ms. Marilyn P. MacCabe, Federal Emergency Management Agency
Mr. John Ortman, United States Department of Energy
Dr. Noel Raufasté, Jr., National Institute of Standards and Technology
Dr. Bill Sacco, Trianalytics Corporation
Mr. Ron Slotkin, United States Environmental Protection Agency
Ms. Linda Straka, Federal Emergency Management Agency

*Montgomery County Public Schools, Rockville, Maryland